Uncommon Sense

In an age when it is 'common sense' to promise much and deliver little, here is a book that does the opposite, delivering much while maintaining a modesty of promise and a down-to-earth voice. It is this kind of 'uncommon sense' that is grist to John G. White's mill.

In *Uncommon Sense: Reclaiming Humanity*, White offers a manual of homespun wisdom, leading the reader along a pathway to health and wholeness, which is an alternative to the ways of the world. At times, the wisdom of this book is reminiscent of that of Wendell Berry, whose *Home Economics* works out many similar themes in a North American setting. White writes out of his Western Australian life experience and work as a psychotherapist and friend and counsellor of prisoners. He knows the ropes; and speaks with a voice that each reader will come to trust, as genuine, honest and reliable. The book is a comprehensive primer in the perennial wisdom of the spirit, which the author counter-poises to the faddish and self-serving ways of the ego.

The book is organised into three broad sections. 1. Foundations of our Humanity, 2. Relating to ourselves and others, and 3. Society's Organisation and beyond. Written in easy bite-size chunks, the author offers summaries of key points at the end of each section. I can see this book being used by individuals seeking a richer, fuller way of life; and groups that wish to explore together the dimensions of the human spirit and the ways of spirituality.

Rev. Dr Geoffrey Lilburne
Author of Joy Interrupted: A Memoir of Depression and Prayer

I have known John White as a close friend for forty years and for several years co-facilitated in prison restorative justice programs with him. I was fortunate enough to be given an Order of Australia in connection with this work but, to be honest, John was at least equally deserving of this award.

As a human being, John is awe inspiring in the breadth of his experience in so many fields (in his cover story he does not even mention the two houses he physically built himself!). I have observed how his enthusiasm and kindly approach have endeared him to generations of people (men, women, children, old folk, the vulnerable, the sick, the prisoner, the powerful – really, anybody). It is an extraordinary gift and has enabled him to explore the humanity of himself and others with their full cooperation. He is widely read, tests out every idea for himself and has sufficient humility to adjust as he attains further insights

The book is clearly the work of a professional, supplemented by a lifetime of experience. There are many original as well as traditional, tried and tested ideas, many of them backed up with short powerful stories that clearly illustrate the principle being shared.

You will be reading wisdom which is the consummation of seven decades of a life well lived.

Michael Cockram AM, LLB.
Retired lawyer

John White is a genuine searching soul, seeking to share the insights he has learnt in his own profound inner journey.

His book comprises an amazing array of diverse gems of wisdom and insight, connected by the themes of helping us to understand who we are and how we can best live our lives in these difficult and troubled times.

Using the wisdom gained from a lifetime of deep study and practice and reflection, he shares a message about the things in life that truly matter; and conveys a way of understanding ourselves and our place in the world that will be deeply helpful to many.

Dr Marie Fox, MB, BS, FRACGP

'Passionate and pacey' I think fairly characterises this elating, frustrating, insightful, outlandishly generalising, poignant book for our times. I feel totally convinced of its central theme: God is love and for the sake of ourselves, our institutions and our planet, love needs to be returned to our central attention, motivation and will. This requires the subordination of the assertive ego to the Spirit.

John White has outlined the content of his own life's values in this didactic, almost sermonic piece. He has integrated classical psychotherapy (Freud, Adler, Frankl and successors) with classical Catholic, Buddhist and Hindu meditative practices and outlook and with a much-needed external perspective on our economic and governance systems.

The spiritual is far too important to be neutered, as much of our wealthy global community would prefer. If you can manage challenge, relish "Uncommon Sense". Otherwise, read it anyway, for it will likely extend your internal library of possibilities for yourself and for society at large.

The Revd. Dr Jeffrey J Sturman,
Retired Anglican priest, Engineer and Environmental Scientist

Having read John White's *Uncommon Sense - reclaiming humanity* from cover to cover, I am glad that readers will be able to dip and re-dip into the various sections listed in the contents as a way of browsing their interests.

I particularly liked Part 2 'Relating to Ourselves and Others' with its accounts of conflict and negotiation, reconciliation and deepening communication among many other topics that present practical and helpful common wisdom.

The book also tackles the 'big questions' of the meaning of life: How shall we live? Who am I? What causes hate, wars, oppression and wholesale destruction? What can we do about it?

Through his 70 plus years of life, much of it as a teacher, psychotherapist, counsellor and spiritual director, John's reflections bring a rare integration of educational knowledge and spiritual values and psychological principles across a range of schools of thought. The distillation in which he has engaged and which he shares brings together not just common sense but uncommon sense and wisdom.

Christabel Chamarette
Clinical Psychologist.

UNCOMMON SENSE

Reclaiming Humanity

JOHN G. WHITE

COVENTRY
PRESS

Published in Australia by
Coventry Press
33 Scoresby Road
Bayswater Vic. 3153
Australia

ISBN 9780987643124

Copyright © John G. White 2019

All rights reserved. Other than for the purposes and subject to the conditions prescribed under the *Copyright Act*, no part of this publication may be reproduced, stored in a retrieval system, or transmitted in any form or by any means, electronic, mechanical, photocopying, recording or otherwise, without the prior permission of the publisher.

Scripture quotations are from the *New Revised Standard Version Bible*, copyright 1989, Division of Christian Education of the National Council of the Churches of Christ in the United States of America. Used by permission. All rights reserved.

And from the Holy Bible, New International Version®, *NIV*®. Copyright © 1973, 1978, 1984, 2011 by Biblica, Inc.™ Used by permission of Zondervan. All rights reserved worldwide. www.zondervan.com The "NIV" and "New International Version" are trademarks registered in the United States Patent and Trademark Office by Biblica, Inc.™

Cataloguing-in-Publication entry is available from the National Library of Australia http:/catalogue.nla.gov.au/.

Cover design by Ian James - www.jgd.com.au
Text by Megan Low, Film Shot Graphics

Printed in Australia

Contents

Introduction	11

Part One:
Foundations of our humanity

Who are we really?	19
Getting reconnected to ourselves: 'religion' redefined	29
Awareness and feelings	39
Who is my life really about?	52
Travelling light	55
Four stages of life	58
Being and doing	63
Belief and its power	66
Psychology, Meaning and Purpose	71
Non-attachment and mindfulness	76

Part Two:
Relating to ourselves and others

Harmony	83
Desire or preference	86
Forgiveness	88
Reconciliation	94
Integrity	101
Games	103
Defending the ego	107
Being Individual and Community	121
Deepening communication	127
Triangles: the geometric traps we build	141
Being a friend	149

The power of thought	153
Conflict and Negotiation	157
Play and Sex	161
Love and Marriage	168
Sex and Language as 'weapons'	176
Support and Challenge	179
How shall we live?	184
Self-responsibility and blaming	203
Interior maintenance: finding wisdom	205

Part Three:
Society's organisation and beyond

Corporatism and the displacement of the citizen	213
Economics	219
Politics or Government?	224
Borders and other arbitrary divisions	231
The trouble with ownership	235
Wealth and Greed	240
Conclusion	243
About the author	245

For the inhabitants of earth

And those who have inspired me with their uncommon 'common sense'

Introduction

When my mum and dad were alive, common sense was 'common'. Life here in Australia – and probably elsewhere from the twenties to the sixties – seemed to be simpler. Most people didn't have more than the essentials required for life to be 'good enough'. I remember business-people in town drove a Holden or Falcon 'special' where most of the other workers had a 'standard' model of some sort. It was only the town doctor who drove a Mercedes Benz and, unless he pranged it (and he pranged a few), he kept it for many years. It was common sense to get the maximum life from goods we had to buy – often at considerable personal sacrifice. It was common sense to consume minimally, to care for and respect everything and everyone. It was common sense generally not to expect, require or demand more than was necessary to live simply and contentedly as a member of a family and community.

Unfortunately, common sense has become uncommon. Hence this little book.

For some years now, I have been increasingly disturbed by the direction we in the West are taking in the living of our lives. I am disturbed by the disastrous impact our way of life is having on the lives of billions of our sisters and brothers in other countries. I am disturbed by our disregard and wholesale destruction of the natural environment of our one and only planet home. Simple has been replaced by complex. Contentment with 'what is' has been replaced by always wanting more. Acceptance of the ordinary has been replaced by desire and demand for the extraordinary. Where once being reasonable was normal, it now seems there is nothing wrong with being unreasonable – especially if you are amongst the wealthy, the loud or the (so-called) powerful.

We used to save in order to make a purchase. Now we acquire everything we want, when we want it, on credit. Where once we put on a scarf, a beanie and an extra layer of clothing, we are now more inclined to turn on a heater. Where once we entertained ourselves with singing around a piano, playing musical instruments, games, talking to one another and reading books, we now turn on the TV, DVD, MP3, X-Box, tablet, smartphone or latest video-game device. Where once we made personal effort to gain new knowledge, acquire new skills, and discover new dimensions in ourselves, we now prefer to sit passively and be spoon-fed whatever the media networks dish up. Where once the citizen was *the legitimate* and honoured unit of society, now it is the corporation. Where once the primary concern was social good for all, now it is economic greed for the few. Where once it was normal to share one's gifts with one's community, now it is normal to guard, accumulate and hoard wealth and knowledge for one's personal benefit. We have moved from profound to profane, from doing 'right' to doing 'what you can get away with', from shame and remorse to denial and arrogance.

This way that we now think and live comes at a great cost to us and to our world. For us, personally, we have to work longer and with less fulfilment to pay for the things we've been led to believe we must have for our lives to be meaningful; for us to be successful, cool or 'with-it'. We have less time and energy to invest in friends and family relationships. Our physical, emotional, mental and spiritual health is seriously compromised. We have more of everything but are less happy than those in cultures who have much less. We talk too much and listen too little. We reject the wisdom of our elders and acknowledged experts, preferring our own opinions. We prefer information to wisdom. We run too much and stroll too little. We prefer noise to silence, movement to stillness. We prefer artificial to natural, complex to simple. We set our minds on the next thing or the previous thing rather than on the present thing. We're designed to live fully, freely and to be life-givers. But, after we've done what we've been led to believe we should do, there is little left in us to give life to ourselves, or anyone or anything else in the world. That is tragic. That is death before we're physically dead.

As for the effect on the only earth we call home – and not only our home but, equally, the home of countless millions of other human beings, other life forms and irreplaceable geological formations – it is being rapidly consumed, polluted, desecrated and destroyed. We are biting the hand that feeds us; killing the very resource that gives us life. There is no sense in that. That is, simply, stupid! We're ramping up the production and burning of coal and gas rather than accelerating the development of clean renewable energy sources. We are playing God by violently fracturing the earth's crust to release coal-seam gas, and poisoning the aquifers that sustain life. We're polluting the earth's waterways, air and land surfaces instead of taking every possible measure to keep them in their natural, pristine, life-supporting states. Our politicians flagrantly dismiss the world's best science and strengthen the lie of 'trickle-down economics'.

Essential services of education, welfare, health and actual community security are degraded in favour of 'growth, greed and wealth' for the 'one-percenters' – the few corporate moguls who actually dictate how our nations are governed. The 'precautionary principle' of good science demands that if we are 'unsure of the outcome, we must not proceed'. That principle is flouted *ad infinitum*. We move plants, animals, soils, water resources to places they were never meant to be, and incur diabolical habitat destruction, pest infestations, crop failures, desertification, salinisation and every other problem associated with messing with nature. And we are intelligent beings! What on earth has happened in order for us to have created this mess? Are there solutions to our problems? If so, what are they? Of course, to focus only on the problems can be depressing and demotivating. A growing number of Australians are doing many good things to interact positively with our environment. There is widening and deepening awareness that we are not separate from the environment but inextricably part of it; care for the earth is care for ourselves and all creatures.

What follows is a collection of awarenesses, strategies, skills, thoughts, beliefs, motivations, new habits (or old ones 're-membered'), etc., that many folk throughout history have found to be essential if we are to get anywhere near the care and contentment in life that we all dream was intended. I'm seventy, now. For about the last thirty-five years in my practice of counselling, psychotherapy, clinical supervision, restorative justice and spiritual direction, I have found these 'truths' transformational in my own life and the lives of hundreds of my clients.

Of course, all this has been said before in various places and ways and you've probably heard most of it too. As it is written in the Bible, for example, *'there is nothing new under the sun'* (Ecclesiastes 1:9). However, the problem I find with helpful information is that when I need it most, I seem to have never learned it or to have forgotten it. If you're anything like normal - that's somewhere under the Bell Curve - you'll probably be a bit the same!

And, by the way, common sense is, literally, a *no-brainer*. It arises from somewhere far deeper within us than our amazing but severely limited 'brains'. One of the problems that we'll deal with later is that we have deified the brain – the intellect. We've allowed ourselves to be deluded into believing that our thinking is our highest function. Wisdom of the ages tells us clearly that it is not. If ancient wisdom isn't sufficiently convincing, take a look around you at the world our intellects have created. Together with the great actions of goodness and life – which, incidentally, arise from that deeper place to which I have alluded – we have endless wars, starvation and oppression. We have gross inequality, violence, greed, pride, arrogance, wholesale destruction of the natural order that sustains all life, and every other malady and evil you might care to mention.

So here's a reminder for you and me of things we all urgently need to learn or relearn and, more than that, act upon, if life on earth is to survive and thrive. And it'll become evident that there are some things we need to unlearn. This is a memory jogger, maybe with something new and useful. It's offered with genuine honour and care for life and for you. I hope you are able to receive it in that way.

John White
Toodyay, Western Australia, 2019

Part One:

Foundations of our humanity

Who are we really?

If we are to make 'sense' common again, where do we start? If we were building a house, we wouldn't start with the interior decoration, roof or walls; we'd start by clearing the site and establishing an appropriate, level, solid foundation. We need the same if we are to build the house of our common humanity so that it stands secure and, yes, magnificent! With the right foundation, we are able to withstand anything life presents to us – the pleasant and the unpleasant. And, strange as it may seem, we need to be able to withstand both. And, more than withstand, we need to *welcome* both, as the pleasant is potentially fatal to us if we don't manage it wisely, and the unpleasant essential to enable us to mature and evolve. More on that later.

In this first section, I hope to provide sufficient explanation of what I believe are the main requirements for a strong foundation. There are many stand-alone points of 'common sense', each having its own merit. But without a secure and believable context in which to ground them, they will merely be 'nice' bits of data immediately enjoyed and quickly lost to us. The only context, the only whole, strong enough to contain the parts must be a sound and accurate understanding of who we really are as human beings at our very core. It will be argued here that we have lost sight of the truth about us. We need to consider the *essence* that will hold all of our *substance*.

We know we are physical bodies made up of cells. Science tells us that, after seven years, there is not one cell in our bodies that was there seven years earlier. So we are not our bodies because they change, disappear and reform continuously. Science also tells us that every atom in our bodies has been through at least three super-novas. That means we are star-dust. We share the properties of everything else in the universe. We are made of the same stuff and we belong with and in and to everything that is. We are also told that in our next breath there will be argon atoms previously breathed by our ancient forebears. We are all powered by the same source of energy. The same breath-energy animates every living being, and we are inextricably caught up in it in an amazing, mysterious yet absolutely real way. There is no way we can escape from our communion with all that is. Even when we die, the material of which we are made remains, but in a transformed state. Here on earth, at least, we live in a finite, closed system. Matter and energy can be changed but not lost. So, here we are. We are stuck with being part of this great, mysterious whole that we know as the universe, and intimately with our beautiful, tiny earth part of it.

We also have minds; we have thoughts and develop beliefs. But they change more often than our underclothes, so we can't be our minds either. And we have feelings and emotions and they, too, change with (often) frightening speed. So we are not our thoughts or feelings. So, what else is there?

Universal wisdom agrees that our essential nature is *spirit*. Never born, never dying, mysterious and ineffable yet more real and secure than anything else in the universe. Made for and in and through that great mystery we know as *love*. And the greatest clue to the fact that, at our core, we *are* love, is that love is the one thing that every single human being desires to experience – to receive and give. We have an inbuilt automatic-direction-finder tuned to the frequency of love. Love, and the inner peace and contentment that accompanies, is the deepest longing of the human heart.

But we don't seem to be very effective at being loving. That is probably because we've mis-defined love as that 'first-love / honeymoon / feeling state' that is merely natural (and wonderful), sensual, sexual attraction and desire. And there's nothing wrong with those. They are essential aspects of our human expression. But they're not the whole story. So, the trouble with our definition or misunderstanding about such experiences, is that they fall well short of satisfying our deepest desire to be 'one with' another and, ironically, with ourselves. They are wonderful at first, pretty good after a while, OK a bit later. But they often end with severe disappointment, hurt, anger and disillusionment with life, love and relationships. But it wasn't love's fault! There's nothing wrong with love! The problem was our misguided expectations of it; our shadow projections onto our chosen partners. If you think you're getting sugar and it turns out to be salt, you're not going to be happy. The task is to find that sugar within ourselves, rather than expecting it to be provided by another. The task is also to realise that there is as much salt in *us* as there is in our partners. More on that later also.

If we begin anything on a false premise, if we build anything on a weak foundation, if we start on a journey not knowing from where it is we start, we cannot begin to navigate a sure passage. Our lives will wander, stumble, crumble, and our activities will be meaningless and worthless. One thing that will almost certainly become evident throughout our investigation of common sense, is that what is often considered successful in life is, in reality, anything but! For example, a government that achieves a surplus budget by allowing health, education and social harmony to degenerate, is a miserable failure. A government – sadly like recent Australian governments – that has succeeded in stopping the arrival of asylum seekers coming in boats, has abjectly failed its international human rights obligation to receive and care for those who are genuine refugees; who are, in fact, our own brothers and sisters! A person who has a spectacular career or who makes a great deal of money, but whose children suffer lack of parental time, love and care, has failed to achieve anything of worth. A sporting hero who develops spectacular physical prowess, but whose personal wisdom, morality and ethics are lacking, achieves nothing. We'll talk more about success in a later chapter.

It is essential that we get the foundation right, or we will not have the resources necessary to comprehend why common sense has become so uncommon, nor will we be able to redress that life-destroying anomaly. We must discover an appropriate understanding of ourselves as human beings if we are to have any chance of living effectively for ourselves, our immediate loved ones, our community of humankind and the beautiful, fragile planet that is home to all creatures.

With some trepidation, here goes!

Universal wisdom generally agrees that there is a single aspect of our nature that trips us up; one essential yet limited quality that most of us fail to adequately understand and manage. I speak of the psychological phenomenon of *ego*, the aspect of our nature that interacts with the external world. The ego contains our senses, thoughts and rational thinking, but doesn't contain all truth. The ego is necessarily strongest when we are young because the presence and function of our *deepest self* has not as yet been developed, understood and acknowledged.

Throughout spiritual literature, this *deepest self* is variously known as 'Spirit, Soul, True Self, Ground of Being, Wisdom, Universal Truth, Atman, God Within', and by many other terms. All these are attempts to name the unnameable; the ineffable mystery of our deepest nature and source of life within us. But, in order to communicate with one another and engage with this mystery, we need a term of some kind to signal what we are attempting to talk about. As any term we choose will have personal associations with any given reader, it is difficult to choose one that will be least misinterpreted.

Now, it is true that there exists substantial agreement amongst most schools of religion and philosophy that the essential nature of a human remains somewhat of a mystery. And mysteries, by definition, cannot be explained. But they can be alluded to by various means. Arguably the most used of those means is the ancient Hebrew term *ruach*, meaning *breath* which is further denoted as *spirit*. Although *homo sapiens* have been around for 100,000 to 200,000 years, from the earliest times of somewhat-enlightened humanity – around 6,000 years ago – the mystery of spirit has been considered the *life-force* within us. By *breath* life is sustained. Trying to make sense of this mystery, early cultural and religious traditions believed this life force to have come from the source of all life, known as the Great Spirit, the Spirit of God, the Holy Spirit Supreme, Brahman, etc. Following from the above, it is perhaps acceptably appropriate for us to consider the mystery of *spirit* as our true essence and the central truth of our being.

Further, it could be said that from this place in us – the centre of wisdom and truth – come animation and right direction for our lives. Scripture states *'it is the spirit that gives life; the flesh counts for nothing'* (John 6:63). This passage – *'the Spirit of truth… will guide you into all the truth'* (John 16:13) – promises that our spirit can have access to the Creator Spirit enabling us to live our best selves.

So, rather than labouring the point, in the interests of simplicity and consistency, to refer to this deepest, wisest, best self, throughout this book, we will use the term *spirit* in the hope that the reader may experience that as referring to the *essential Centre, the animating principle,* the *profound, mystical reality* of their person. If we can accept that the Creator Spirit is both providing and communicating life to us, and we are willing to embrace that truth, then for *spirit* we can also read *'that place in us in which guidance is revealed for the purpose of carrying out appropriate executive function of my person'*. The spirit in us is the location of truth.

Although it is inaccurate to call any aspect of our person 'false' – because each aspect is a real part of us – it is necessary to differentiate the 'shallow' from the 'deep' so to speak. Even those two terms are subjective and not as helpful as we might like. However, we need some way to proceed. So, for the purposes of this discussion, I hope it will suffice to separate the 'higher self' from the 'lower self' – the *spirit* from what we will call the *ego*. Let's try to clarify this difficult matter.

The function of the ego is to give us boundaries and limits to keep us safe as we experiment with life's various aspects. The ego is that part of us that acquires knowledge and skill, relates to the environment and to other people and creatures, and generally interacts with the external, physical world on a day to day basis. The ego is good and essential much of the time when we are young, and at many times throughout life. But the limited ability of the ego must be understood and transcended if we are to become mature, adult beings.

As we've discussed above, fortunately the ego has a companion; a companion far wiser than itself and whose rightful role is to function as the *executive* of the person. It is arguable that all the problems of humanity can be traced to the ego's lack of awareness; lack of consciousness. One deficit in awareness is that we believe we're nothing more than *ego*. A second deficit is that we are aware we have a *spirit*, but refuse to submit to it; refuse to surrender the ego to the *spirit* who, alone, is able to effectively function as executive.

Alcoholics Anonymous is one of the great movements in history enabling people to gain some control of their addictions. And we all have many addictions to deal with other than alcohol or drugs, and equally as dangerous to the welfare of the Soul. And one step in A-A is to 'surrender to a higher power'. That power may be termed 'God'. Whatever the name, the power is within us but beyond the function of the ego. That higher power can be thought of as present in us as spirit; the authentic, 'essential' you and me. And for that reason – because it is of far greater importance and power than the ego – it is the Centre of our being from which we *must* learn to live.

But the ego is practised, habituated, arrogant – or well-meaning but unaware – and is reluctant to give up control to anyone or anything else. Part of the reason for that is that, throughout our early years, we have not been adequately taught that we have a spirit. Or, better still, that we *are* spirit inhabiting a physical, emotional, intellectual body. Schools have generally focused on developing the mind and the body. They have also emphasised kindness, generosity, compassion, respect, acceptance and a host of other excellent qualities. The problem is that the resources to enable those qualities to become centrally established in our attitudes and actions have not been readily accepted or developed. Why? Because most of our systems – including the education system – are more influenced by the action of the ego and mind than by the action of the spirit. Unless we are submitted and surrendered, we are unable to model, encourage and teach others that way of being. You cannot teach or inculcate authentic respect or honour for another being if you have not surrendered to, and become one with, the source of that honour. To attempt to teach it as a concept of the mind and even as an intention is to root it too shallowly. In the face of the first serious challenge, it will founder. Only when honourable, true, human, divine qualities are grounded in the essence or spirit of the person, can they withstand all challenges and overcome all that is less than they.

As we open ourselves to widely and deeply consider what it means to be human and living on this planet, we must consider the use of every aspect of our humanity. This will necessarily require that we use not only our minds, but also our hearts, our bodies and, most importantly, our spirits. To become wise, we need to search comprehensively. We must consider what is said about us by scientific, social, relational, emotional, psychological, philosophical and, most importantly, spiritual traditions throughout the history of the human race.

Uncommon sense

- We are made of the same stuff as the universe, and belong with and in and to everything that is.
- We are all powered by the same source of Spirit energy.
- At our core, we are spirit.
- The ego is that part of us containing the senses, mind and reason but not all truth. It acquires knowledge and skill, relates to the environment and to other people and creatures, and generally interacts with the external world on a day to day basis.
- The ego has a companion far wiser that itself, and whose rightful role is to function as the executive of the person. We will call this the spirit.
- The ego is habituated but unaware. Its desire is to keep us safe and, thinking it is doing so, is reluctant to give up control of the person.
- 'We are not physical beings having a spiritual experience; we are spiritual beings having a physical experience.' (Pierre Teilhard de Chardin)
- It is arguable that much of the trouble in our lives and world can be traced to the action of the unaware ego.
- For us to function effectively as mature human beings, we must gain a correct understanding of who we really

are, what makes our lives work, and how we are to live that is good for us, for all other beings and for the earth.

Getting reconnected to ourselves: 'religion' redefined

Don't read that dreaded word 'religion' and panic; what follows is not what you might think!

To continue our consideration of an appropriate and functional understanding of who we are, we need to deal with a major impasse. We find that, as we come into contact with anything in life, we are either more or less comfortable, depending on our experience and understanding. The things with which we are least comfortable are almost certainly those things that need most of our attention. One of the least comfortable is likely to be that of religion. Religion is an issue about which many people get twitchy, because it is an issue that, somehow inside ourselves, we know we need to deal with. Somehow.

The simplest way to deal with any twitchiness is to consider what religion *actually* means and, particularly, what it does *not* mean! This discussion is made necessary because religion has been so distorted and mismanaged over aeons that it generally bears little resemblance to the Truth to which it points.

If it is true that human beings are, at essence, spiritual beings inhabiting a physical body for a few years, then there is nothing more important than to get a correct understanding of what that actually means. We need to understand – as much as we are able to – who we really are, what makes our lives work, how we are to live that is good for us, for all other beings and for the planet. Anyone uncomfortable about religion? Excellent! Let's start with that. Let's consider what religion *doesn't* mean and what it *does*. If we come to a correct understanding, all our fear will dissolve, and we will be released from the burden of avoiding, resisting, being afraid, angry and argumentative about the subject. And we'll be able to easily accept ourselves and all others with equanimity, with peace and contentment, and an experience of freedom. And speaking about freedom, someone once said that *'freedom is release from the intolerable burden of having to have your own way'*. This, of course, is referring to the ego making appropriate way for the wise, executive - working of the spirit.

So, what does religion *not* mean. It doesn't mean belief in a God who is watching and keeping score of the good and bad things we do and either rewarding us or punishing us. It doesn't mean adhering to a set of rules and regulations designed to spoil our joy. It doesn't mean attending activities of a 'religious' nature. It doesn't mean saying certain words, thinking certain thoughts, singing certain songs. It has nothing to do with human-made organisations that control the way we live. It doesn't mean merely going to church, temple, synagogue, mosque or any other meeting place. It is not exclusive but inclusive. It is not arrogant or proud. It never exercises control over anyone. It enforces no demands and makes no judgments. It is not unkind or impatient. It is not rude or self-centred. It is not angry and doesn't keep score of wrongs. It is not something of which to be afraid. In fact, if we are afraid to any extent, we are not religious, because true religion results in the exact opposite of fear, i.e. love!

So what does religion mean? Here are some ideas to consider.

The word 'religion' needs to be redefined. It has come to be much misunderstood and those who claim to highly value the 'concept' seem to allow and, even prefer, this misunderstanding to persist.

If we can engage a person – any person – with genuine interest in and personal regard for them, we will soon find that everyone is actually seeking 'religion'. What they are not interested in – nor am I – is the less than useful machinations of some aspects of religious organisations and many of the associated beliefs, requirements and activities. Much religion as we know it is, by default, actually doing the opposite of that for which it believes itself to stand. I think humanity will make little real progress until we either find another term, or redefine the term 'religion' to again mean what it actually means. And then engage with it.

And speaking of another term, 'spirituality' doesn't seem to be much better because it has become to mean almost anything any individual wants it to mean. Oil and mining companies polluting and destroying eco-systems even talk about their spirituality. Child abusers, thieves, con-men (there may also be con-women) believe they have a spirituality. Corporate bosses, capitalist ladder-climbers, sects and fad-followers of all descriptions boast of 'their personal spirituality', their 'private faith' and use other lame excuses for not submitting to anything greater than their little egos. Spirituality could become a useful term but, it, too, would have to be redefined. And, if it were, it would look remarkably similar to redefined religion. So let's not duplicate effort. Let's consider redefining religion. In my limited ability, let me try to explain.

If we go back to the main roots in Latin, we'll find a couple of terms to which 'religion' is related.

The first is 'religare'. 'Re' means 'again'. 'Ligare' means 'to bind'. So 'religare' means 'to bind again'. Unfortunately for us, this sense of 'binding' has gained the negative connotation of 'having an obligation placed upon one'. Now we all know that the human person is made for freedom and naturally resists any suggestion of being bound. And rightly so.

The second – although not directly related but helpfully supportive – is 'relegere'. This again comprises two words meaning 'to read again'. The implications are several: first, 'you haven't got it: read it again'. A second may be, when you do really 'get it', it doesn't remain; we have to revisit daily for our lifetime. 'Read it' again and again. Don't ever stop returning to it to know it better and better and deeper and deeper. As a musician doesn't stop practising once they have become expert, we can't stop once we 'get' what religion is really about. Of course, what you 'read again and again' is crucial. Obviously, we are talking about Wisdom literature; scriptures and other profound, spirit-focused writings accepted throughout millennia as truth about us.

The problem is that, in the minds of many, religion has come to mean 'there's a supreme being called "God" who has a big stick and is in the business of spoiling our fun, demanding that we do what he requires, and belting us if we get it wrong'. That couldn't be further from the reality. If 'God' is anything (and God is just a word we use to refer to an entity impossible to accurately describe or understand), God is Love. And we're not talking Hollywood here.

If we consider for a moment the primary heart's desire of every ordinary, reasonably right-minded person, we hear the word 'love'. It seems to be what we all intrinsically know to be the most necessary and favoured state of being human. We all want to be loved, and we all want someone to love. And when we achieve that blissful state – even for a moment – life seems to make sense and to work. Why is this so? Could it be that love is our true nature calling from the depths of our inner being? There are plenty of major religious and philosophical paradigms that agree with this basic belief, as do I.

The trouble is, life has become profane. We have become intellectually clever and technologically sophisticated. We have fallen into the error of thinking that we are able to control everything in our lives. And, worse, that these wonderful, new abilities of ours are, in fact, who we are! Therein lies the problem. Our deepest nature - that mysterious, ineffable, God-quality we call spirit, the fount of 'love' – has been relegated to the backseat and is no longer able to exert the influence required for life to work correctly.

If this is so, what humanity actually needs is 'religion' in the truest sense of 'reading again' and being 'bound' to the truth of what it means to be human – i.e. a 'Being'-in-Love'; to know that we are fully human and alive only as we put love first; to seek love before all else. People the world over through all time willingly abandon themselves to one another when love is present. Willingly 'bind' themselves, if you like. The message here? When love is present, 'binding' yourself to it is the smartest, most freeing thing to do. There is no sense of obligation. And if there were, we would accept that willingly anyway because this love promises a state of being that is unquestionably the most desirable there is. Secure, trustworthy, hopeful, enduring, blissful.

Those two terms, 'religare' and 'relegere', are found at the centre of many religious paths. We hear of being 'born again', 'waking up', becoming 'enlightened', reaching 'nirvana', etc. – all terms to do with 'reading again', 'seeing afresh', 'seeing correctly'. Being 'bound' again to the journey into truth, love, wisdom, spirit. To Oneness with all that is, re-joining our place of belonging, returning to the right state of being', etc., etc. Such 'seeing and being' does not carry the burdensome sense of being obligated and controlled by some all-powerful deity. Rather, it has the sense of being liberated into the light of love and truth. Being released from the suffering wrought by being *actually* bound and deceived by the lie that we (our egos) are sufficient within ourselves to order our little lives. Being liberated and enabled to experience peace which is our natural state as 'reconnected' beings. We need to not get hung up on the word 'God'. This is just the word we use for love, light, truth, wisdom, true freedom, bliss, contentment – any such word you may call to mind to refer to being in the most desirable and workable state possible. But it is true that in order to find our 'true' life, we have to lose our 'false' life (or, at least, relegate it to the back seat). We can't have both.

Most of us who are seeking religion as I have defined it above, also want to hang onto the ego structures and their imagined benefits with which we have become so comfortable. It can't be done. We can't have one foot on the pier and the other on the yacht that is setting sail. If we want the real thing, we have to be all in. And letting go of the familiar is the hardest task for the ego, because it has always been in control, and is fearful of what may happen to it if it lets go to the unknown. The fact is every future moment is unknown to the ego – and to the spirit, for that matter – so holding on for the illusion of security is a futile act. There is no security as we define it in this life. The only true security, the only true peace, contentment and meaningful existence, is to be experienced in complete surrender of the ego to the spirit. *'We have no rest until we find our rest in God'* (Augustine of Hippo)

Therefore our task of 'selling' religion (to ourselves first, of course) is really an easy one. We are selling what we and others are already desperate for but didn't know it by that name. Successful marketing and selling is about branding. When we re-brand religion appropriately as *'reading again, seeing correctly and being actually freed by voluntarily "binding" ourselves to that correct way of being'*, religion will sell itself, and many of the problems of humankind will simply fall away. There can be no restoration of the brokenness of the world, its creatures and its people unless we re-engage with religion as it truly is; unless we *re-link* to all that we are within ourselves and, thus, relink to all others and all parts of the created order.

And whilst we're considering the centrality of religion, we need to avoid the arrogance of believing that we have the 'right' take on religion. To make such a claim is always to be divisive – no matter how close to being right we may be, always limiting, always alienating. It is sobering, humbling – and unifying – to realise that we don't know what we don't know. True religion is inclusive, life-giving and creative, not alienating, adversarial and destructive. And I encourage us all to avoid any person who dogmatically claims to have a monopoly on the truth. Not only will they 'do your head in' and turn you off your quest, they will likely 'do your soul in' as well. That is the greatest tragedy imaginable.

Now, if we've managed to accept the argument above, and are willing to move on to this new way of being, I encourage us to simply do the following: thank the ego for its committed service to this point. I'm serious! This is important. The ego is a bit like a child, and its feelings can be easily hurt. So, to simply abandon it – reject it 'after all I've done for you', etc. – in favour of the new kid on the block (the spirit), it is likely to sulk and renew its efforts to undermine future work towards increasing wholeness. Your ego has been faithfully endeavouring to keep you safe from all the dangers of the external world and keep you feeling strong, significant and in control. Recognition of its good service is to honour the good in its function. Then invite it to take a vacation, and advise it that its demanding role of being in control is now complete. It can confidently hand over that task to the spirit who is now to be the appropriate executive of this life. In taking this kind of approach, you are already eliminating the adversarial aspect of intra-action within the person, and demonstrating gently but powerfully the new *modus operandi*. If the ego believes that its person is in safe hands of this 'new executive', it will relinquish its hold on power and the transition will be achieved with minimal angst.

As we practise – as we learn to listen to and submit to this spirit – we experience a kind of release; like a load lifted off. We no longer have to hold on. Rather, we are being held onto. It seems easier to manage being alive. The first thing you may notice, is a growing and increasing awareness of things both outside you and within. Colours, forms, aromas, textures, sounds, etc. may seem clearer, sharper, richer. This is because the energy you (ego) have been using to survive is now available to be redeployed to tasks that are more to do with thriving than merely surviving. And you will notice your inner experience is also transforming. You will be more aware of what others are saying rather than thinking what you will say next. You'll be more relaxed and present. And this is just the beginning. This awareness needs ongoing, vigilant practice and development.

Uncommon sense

- To engage appropriately with the concept of religion, we need to consider what religion actually means and what it does not mean.

- Religion has been so distorted over time that it generally bears little resemblance to the truth to which it points. Much religion as we know it is, by default, actually doing the opposite of that for which it believes itself to stand.

- If it's true that, at essence, humans are spiritual beings inhabiting a physical body for a few years, nothing is more important than to get a correct understanding of what that actually means.

- Religion comes from the Latin term 'religare' – to 'bind again'; to 'relink' (to Truth)

- If 'God' is anything, God is 'love'.

- Our primary desire is to receive and give love. Why? Could it be that love is our True Nature calling from the depths of our inner being? From our spirit?

- Our problems are the result of our becoming so intellectually clever and technologically sophisticated that we believe that's all we are and that we can control everything in our lives.

- Life on earth desperately needs religion in the truest sense of being 'bound again' to truth / love.

- When love is present, 'binding' yourself to it is the smartest, most freeing and blissful thing to do.

- True religion is 'seeing correctly'. Such seeing does not carry the burdensome sense of being obligated and controlled by some all-powerful deity. Rather, it has the sense of being liberated into the light of love and truth.

- The only true security, the only true peace, contentment and meaningful existence, is to be experienced in complete surrender of the ego to the spirit.

- There can be no restoration of the brokenness of the world, its creatures and its peoples, unless we re-engage with religion as it truly is; unless we re-link to all that we are within ourselves and, thus, re-link to all others and all parts of the created order.

- True religion is inclusive, life-giving and creative, not alienating, adversarial and destructive.

- We no longer have to hold on. Rather we are being held onto.

Awareness and feelings

As we allow the spirit in us to be our guide, we become increasingly aware of all that is happening within us and around us. We move from unconsciousness to consciousness. From unawareness to awareness.

So what is *awareness* and what's its place in life?

Anthony de Mello – a great, contemporary, recently-deceased master of sensible religion and spirituality, psychology and philosophy – deals with this topic in a playful yet profound manner in his excellent little book titled *Awareness* (Doubleday, NY, 1990). It has become one of my favourite companions and I re-read it regularly. I encourage you to read it if you haven't. It is about 'waking up'. De Mello delightfully states in the beginning of his book that *'spirituality* (religion 'redefined') *means waking up. Most people, even though they don't know it, are asleep. They're born asleep, they live asleep, they marry in their sleep, they breed children in their sleep, they die in their sleep without ever waking up'*. A challenging statement? Let's open it up a bit.

In his book, de Mello differentiates between the 'I' and the 'me' referring to the 'Self' (capital 'I', spirit to which I refer above) and the 'ego' (lower case 'me'). Christian religion relates these in terms of 'the old man/woman' and the 'new man/woman', i.e. the unregenerate person and the regenerate person. The unaware and the aware. Buddhism uses the terms 'unenlightened' and 'enlightened', and various other expressions of spirituality talk about 'attached' and 'non-attached' for the same issue. The ego is attached, linear, either/or. The spirit is non-attached, circular, 'both-

and'. The spirit reality and practice of non-attachment will be a theme throughout this book, as non-attachment is *the way* of the maturing adult person. To remain attached is to remain in the merciless and destructive operation of the ego and will never result in mature personhood and enlightenment. Nor will it result in a life of significant worth to itself or others.

Once we are aware that we are more and deeper than we previously thought, we can begin healthy self-observation. This is not to say self-absorption. The former is of the spirit; the latter of the ego. Learning and practising self-observation is to become familiar with our inner workings. What am I thinking, feeling, doing and what is causing all this? It's about watching yourself. For example, have you ever had the experience of saying something to someone, and then saying to yourself *'what on earth did I say that for'*? Who is talking to whom here? It seems there are two selves inside you. And you are right. The ego and the spirit; the 'me' and the 'I'. And it is generally the 'I' who says to the 'me' *'what on earth did I say that for'*. So watching what is going on inside us, listening to what we are saying, feeling and doing, is the way to authentic, aware, profound humanity. Awareness is deep presence to, and understanding of, our thoughts, words, feelings and actions.

You may have heard the story of the young woman who cuts off the leg of the roast before putting it in the oven to cook. Her daughter asks her *'Mum, why do you cut the leg off'*? Mum answers *'I've always done it this way as my mother did it.'* The daughter asks grandma the same question. Grandma answers, *'Because, my dear, I only had a small oven and the roast wouldn't fit in unless I cut the leg off'*. Understanding what we do and why is important. Otherwise, we just drift through life asleep, never knowing what we're doing and why, and never being awake; never being conscious.

Awareness is more about *unlearning* than it is about learning something new. When we become aware of what we think, say, do and why, if the reasons are not sound, we unlearn them; we drop them. To knowingly continue to do the same things day after day without knowing why is insane. Asleep. Unaware. We are breathing and moving but we're dead.

When we're aware, we are in charge of our emotional life because we at last understand that *our feelings are our responsibility*. To say *'you made me feel angry'* is insanity. Where are your feelings of anger? Inside you! They are yours. You create them. They arise in and belong to you. Of course it is normal to react emotionally to input from outside ourselves. But no one but you creates your emotional experience.

Here's how it happens in the unenlightened, 'old me'. You want someone to like you and they don't, so you feel hurt. But they didn't hurt you; your unfulfilled wanting is what caused your pain. YOU caused it! Don't blame anyone else. Blame your own wanting. The Buddha said, *'all suffering is caused by desire'*. Your wanting and your not getting caused you to suffer. The solution: stop wanting! Stop desiring! It's in your control. Or at least be aware of your desiring and the hurt you felt as a result. That is the beginning of being aware, conscious, awake.

It is a beautiful thing to be aware. It feels powerful and hopeful. You are no longer at the mercy of people's opinions, words and actions. You create your own responses. Someone said *'what other people think of me is none of my business'*. I like that. *Your* opinion of you is the only one worth anything to you; the only one you can easily live with. Of course, it is always good to *reflect* on what others say about us, and then either accept their opinion (and modify our behaviour), or reject it.

Do read de Mello's book. It's a gem on the road to being free, to be the magnificent individual you were designed to be, both for your benefit and for that of your community to which you are to contribute. Remember the 'I' and the 'me', listen to the voices inside you and choose to respond from the wise one; the 'I'. To react from the 'me' is to have your emotional life and, thus, your whole life, driven this way and that by every external event that crosses your path, every opinion, statement, non-verbal experience.

Life is valuable and we only have one. It makes no sense to allow someone or something else to determine its quality and effectiveness. We need to choose what is of real value to us, to others and to the earth. First, we need to be aware what the options are from which to choose.

All over the world, mines are running out of minerals, wells are running out of oil and gas, the atmosphere is running out of ozone, forests are running out of trees, animals, birds and insects, and oceans are running out of fish. Depressing, isn't it? We've been beavering away in the external world depleting it as fast as we can. And the internal world of 'you' and 'I' has hardly had a look in. Because when we do, we are scared of what we see and don't know what on earth (or in heaven) to do about it! And here's the rub! The greatest resource on the planet is virtually untapped. It is accessible to everyone equally, it is impossible to exhaust because the supply is self-generating and eternal. And yet, we in our cleverness have scorned it as somehow second rate and have denied ourselves and future generations the glorious benefits of it. Instead, we have preferred gruel and brackish water when we could have had caviar and champagne! And we think we are intelligent. I find it hard to reconcile that.

What am I talking about? What's this great resource? It's too simple to say that it's awareness. But certainly awareness is the way to it. The resource is Truth, essence of life, foundation or ground of being, spirit, Love. Now that may sound cute and religious and warm and fuzzy and all that. And because we discount love as somehow less sophisticated than information or knowledge or manipulation of the material world, we have cut off our noses to spite our faces. How many times have you heard a boardroom-type comment like *'let's not get emotional about this; we must be rational'*. As if being rational is the greatest good in humanity. What a tragedy! Being rational is placed above being true!

Friend, we are in deep trouble! Feel what is valued in our society. Listen to what politicians base all their policies on. Get a taste for what commercial media focuses on. Look at what people watch on TV. Experience how traditional values of family and small community have been eroded until they are almost non-existent. But don't despair! All is well! We just need to make some adjustments to humanity. Starting with our own. Those adjustments are life shaking but simple. The trouble is, we don't want the only solution there is. We want another solution. A more comfortable one. A solution that doesn't ask too much of us or change our life too much. Can't be done.

With cancer, radical surgery is often required to heal. With a full-term pregnancy, radical, tissue-wrenching delivery of one from another is required for life to continue. To get life back on track after illegal or immoral activity, awareness of error associated with deep remorse, an about-face and, often, restitution is required to effect the change. These are not easy things I'm talking about. They are simple, but they are difficult because they require facing who we really are; all the glory and all the filth because, in reality, that's who we all are, and it's all ok! When we have at least a beginning awareness of that truth, we are able to heal and change and become who we were meant to be in the first place.

One of the hard things about this topic is to stick with it. To be dealt with effectively, ideas and terms and behaviours must be embraced which are roundly denounced these days. But truth is truth. If you want it, prepare to be challenged. Some of your sacred- or not-so-sacred cows will need to die. And prepare to be on your own. This journey into life is one that few seem to take. Companions on the way are often hard to find. But this path – even completely bereft of human company if that's what it comes to – is experienced as delightful, and one you wouldn't dream of trading for anything.

But, before we get into what may be a challenge for you, let me attempt some support. Hopefully, this will be experienced by you as genuine and sensitive, for that is my intent. And I need to be careful, because often my passion gets the better of my sensitivity. I run the risk of being like a bulldozer. My dear old dad was, too, come to think of it.

John G. White

The first thing to say here is that I have no ground to judge your ideas and beliefs. They are precious to you, have probably been hard won and are as valid as anyone's. You have feelings about your ideas and values that are probably quite deep and powerful, and that's how it should be. That's normal. No one has the right to discount your feelings or beliefs. No one has the right to put themselves and their ideas above yours. No one has the right to deal with you in any way other than to respect you as an equal. I hope you can hear that and experience what is coming from me as doing that very thing. If I can't convey that in these few words, please forgive my clumsiness and bear with me. What's *most* important is to bear with yourself. Trust sufficiently in yourself not to be put off or put down or put somewhere by me or anyone else.

Start from where you are. It's the only place you can be right now anyway, and it's as good a place as any. But don't be content to stay there. Whatever 'good and wise' you and I have found, there is more. Don't settle for less than the best a human can have or be. Stay with me as we consider some of these fundamentals of our humanity that have a life and death effect on us. And I mean that literally. There are lots of walking dead in the world. Probably most of us are. I'll develop this a bit as we go.

Someone far wiser than me said this. And it in no way denigrates the profound value of each of our parts, our endeavours, or of the windows through which we view life. But it does rearrange them in a different priority order. Here it is.

'*Science is the lowest form of human endeavour because science deals with matter and uses discursive thought. Above science is philosophy because philosophy deals with ideas, and ideas are of a higher order than matter. But philosophy still uses discursive thought. Above philosophy is religion because religion deals with transcendent ideas, which are higher order than ordinary ideas. But religion still uses discursive thought. Above religion is Truth which is above all ideas and intellectual ability. It can only be engaged by abandoning discursive thought, by acknowledging the finiteness of the ego self, by surrendering all of that self, and opening your heart, your centre, to the mystery.* (Bede Griffiths: *Return to the Centre*)

How do we deal with that? If we can, how do we do it? Simply but with difficulty because of who we are and how hard we cling to the little things of our little lives. And how fixed we are in our habitual ways of being that have allowed no room for ways that better serve us all. Amongst the ways of being for which we have made too little space, and on which we have placed too little value, are these: meditation, prayer, contemplation, stillness, silence, practising non-attachment by whatever means, letting go of the life we know to embrace the life we long for. Jesus says, *"lose your life to find it"* and *"die to self in order to live"* and *"the last will be first"* and *"if you would be great, be the servant of all"* and many other instructions that sound crazy and, to our human minds and egos, are. But the human mind is not the last word about life. In our ignorance and/or arrogance, we have come to think it is. *We have to courageously accept the reality that the mind of God, of Truth, of Eternal Spirit is far greater and diametrically opposed to most of what is commonly accepted by the rest of the world* as right. Oscar Wilde said, 'When someone agrees with me, I rethink my position'. He may have been a little extreme but the point is to be made; populism is to be considered with great suspicion.

I'm taking the premise that the above statement is true and that we need to leave what's familiar in our little lives of manipulating the world of material and ideas, and risk engaging with – re-linking (because that's what religion actually means) - to the Great Story, the Truth about us. Are you game to go on? You've got all the resources you need right inside you, you know? The Bible says that *"the Kingdom of God is within you"* Can you get the magnitude of that? All the power and wisdom and resource of the Creator and creation is in you and me! That's enough to blow the average mind. And what we're more afraid of than the *darkness* inside us is the *light;* the glory to which I have just alluded. How wonderful it would be if we were all to get in touch with the amazing reality about us. Nothing would be impossible. Nothing would hold us back. No evil would be able to stand against us. The world and all its people would be transformed.

Now, maybe I've already challenged the core of your beliefs about life by mentioning religion. If you don't accept that there's a greater power than yourself, we can't go much further. But, if that's the case, before you abandon this line of reflection, read on for a while. I've got some information and some experiments I'd like you to consider before you throw all this out.

One of the experiments is this. Can you honestly say that there is no longing inside you for something more? Can you honestly say that you are completely satisfied, content, joyful, secure and powerful? Can you honestly say that you are just matter and that when you die that's the end of it all.

Inside every human being is a deep longing, a deep hunger for something more. No one is exempt. We can stave it off for years. We can pretend it doesn't exist. We can ridicule it in others. We can avoid, justify, rationalise, intellectualise, minimise and every other kind of 'ise' there is. But we can't get rid of it. As you read these words, you know it is true of you. Human beings were made for union with the mystery of God who made them. God's plan is that this inner longing can only be satisfied by union of the individual spirit with the Spirit of God. We can argue against this all our life. We can want it to be different. We can embrace any other religion or philosophy you like. Nothing will change the reality that the God plan – the spirit journey – is the only one that is workable. It is similar with other universal laws. Gravity, for example: we can refuse to believe in gravity but we can't change it. We can only demonstrate it.

Our western governments are continually looking for programs and spending endless amounts of money to end drug use, crime and lawlessness generally. They are trying to use external strategies to solve an internal sickness. The governments in Israel and Palestine are doing the same. The famines and oppressions all around the world are trying to do the same. And yet the solution, the only solution, is an inner one. The heart of humankind is what needs changing. When the heart of man and woman changes, love replaces fear and hate. Enemies no longer exist. Only brothers and sisters. That's the truth I'm trying to get us to engage here. That's the only truth that is any good to us. That's at the heart of awareness. There is no option. We either become aware of this great reality, or we remain dead. Economics hasn't solved it. Politics hasn't solved it. Philosophy hasn't solved it. 'Organised religion' hasn't solved it. Only truth will work. That's what we have to become aware of. I encourage us all not to settle for less. We *are fearfully and wonderfully made* and our task is to realise that wonder in its designed context.

So, let's try to get a feeling for this thing called awareness; see what it looks like. Listen to a few word ideas. Awareness is watching yourself, observing yourself - not in a preoccupied or self-obsessive way, not evaluating or judging or criticising, just observing; watching. Seeing, hearing, tasting, touching, smelling what's there. Being *you* as you are, and being in touch with that *you* through your senses. That's awareness. Quiet, still, ordinary observation of yourself. *'I'm feeling hot. I'm aware of some anxiety in me. I can hear the magpies carolling, smell the lemon-scented gums since the rain, taste the tannins in the new wine, see the pale golden wash on the horizon of the eastern sky at dawn'.* Just watch your experience without evaluating, interfering, judging. Just noticing, accepting, being with whatever is happening at any given time. And watch your reactions too. Don't evaluate them. Just notice them. Awareness is somewhere in all this. And when we are aware, we are connected to all that we are and all that the universe is with its everyone and everything for all time. We are not separated. We belong. We're *religious* (re-linked), undivided, at one with all things and all people. And, because there is no longer me and something or someone else but all is in communion, attachment no longer has any meaning. Attachment takes two or more entities and there is but *one* now. Because there is no attachment, there is no disharmony, no enmity, no anxiety, no alienation. All is well. There is peace. Joy.

When we live in such a state, the only reality is love through which, by which and for which we are created and only in which can we function as we were intended. There is no truly human/religious experience without such a state. In such a state, there can be no wars, no famines, no oppression, no pain, no hatred, no fear. Only love. The one truth and power of the universe. Lose yourself to find yourself. Die to live. Leave to find. Give to receive. All the paradoxes rest in harmony here. Awareness. Become aware. Become conscious. Function in harmony with yourself and others. That's living. Anything else is just existing and, more accurately, walking death.

Uncommon sense

- The greatest resource – love/truth – is inside us. Don't search anywhere else.
- Rational is irrational (foolishness, immaturity).
- Spirit has been traded for trinkets. If we think life as we know it is wonderful, it's a pale and pathetic whisper of what was meant to be.
- Re-linking – re-connecting – (re-ligion) to the real Self is required for healing life and the planet.
- There's a greater power than you and me (thank God)!
- Science, philosophy and organised religion are just the beginning. Truth is beyond them all.
- Meditation, prayer, contemplation, silence, stillness are some of the ways to the Way.
- Whether we like it or not (and the sooner we get to accept it the easier life will be for us all), the truth is

spirit in me created, enlivened and informed by the Spirt of God, Supreme Spirit.

- Awareness is watching, observing yourself – without judgment, evaluation, criticism.
- Awareness leads to One-ness.
- Leave the self to find the Self.

Who is my life really about?

As we become increasingly aware, we soften all previous beliefs and attitudes, and are more comfortable with not knowing and not needing to know in the usual sense. The boundaries we lived within collapse, and we are open to considering life more freely and contentedly. What we thought was fact, we're now not so sure. And we don't care anyway.

Here's another challenging statement. Your life's not really about you - entirely. Of course, it may not be true, but I suspect it is. Someone once said there are five things you need to know about life before you really start living:

Life is hard. (We all know that...)

You're going to die. (Yep, got that one too)

You've got no control over pretty much everything (bummer)

You're not that important anyway – well, important, but no more so than any other human being.

Your life's not even about you

What do we make of that? Well, the first three are pretty obvious and most of us accept those as true. The fourth point, I suspect, we all feel at some stage. We have an inner longing to be significant, yet we have a sneaking suspicion we're not. And that causes some distress. Probably the truth is that we *are* and we *aren't* very important. First, we are because we are a human being equal in worth to every other human being ever – whether we feel that or not. We each have a worth – a value – of '1'. It is logical that as we are all human beings with all the same bits, we are all are worth the same. Of course, the world will tell us that some are worth more than others because of their intellect, their beauty, their skill, their contribution to the human effort, the money they have. But these are just ego judgments of fallible people and don't necessarily carry any truth. Whilst our judgments are limited to our senses, mind and reason, they are almost always inadequate.

And we are not important in that we are just one of the great mob, no more, no less than any other. And, therefore, although we are as important, logically we are not *very* important!

But the fifth 'truth' – 'your life's not even about you' – needs some unpacking. If my life's not about me, then who is it about? Well, as none of us can fully live in isolation – we have needs for companionship, assistance, guidance, protection, and needs to love and serve and give – we belong to the group; the group needs us and we need them. So it is arguable that our lives belong to the whole rather than to one part, i.e. 'me'. It is also demonstrable that when we are in relationship, our lives are experienced as having greater meaning, purpose, pleasure (and pain), security, provision, creativity, etc. And, not only do we belong to the whole of humanity, but to the whole of the natural order in which we function, of which we are made, and on which we have marked effect! So when we are able to accept this outrageous idea that our lives are not about us, we can relax on some matters, not take ourselves so seriously, and become more appropriately focused in other matters to moderate our impact on earth-life generally. And life becomes easier, more manageable, more pleasant. The need to achieve a certain outcome is no longer a pressure, the need to impress is no longer there, we do have roles of significance to play, and we simply *are*. And all is well enough.

Uncommon sense

- Life is hard: accept it and get on with it. Stop expecting it to be easy. Make an effort, not an excuse.

- You're going to die. If you don't embrace that fact, you'll live in constant anxiety about something you have no hope of changing.

- You've got no control. When you accept that, and give up trying to control, you will experience peace in simply 'being'. You'll be free. Someone once said, *'freedom is release from the intolerable burden of having to have your own way'*. There's great wisdom in that.

- You're not really important anyway. When you stop wanting to be important and accept that you're not and never will be, as if by magic you'll feel relieved, relaxed, unburdened and, strangely, important! It's the 'wanting', the 'desire' that causes all our suffering.

- Your life's not even about you only. When you are able to rest in the above four points, little 'you' won't matter so much to you anymore, and you'll be free to go out of yourself to others and – again as if by magic – you will experience your life as being meaningful and wonderful.

- So please sit, breathe, be present, change anything you are able to, accept anything you are unable to change. Realise you belong to the great whole of humanity and creation, that you are a meaningful part of all that is, and all is well. All will begin to be experienced as well. More magic!

Travelling light

As we get clearer about who we are and are not, and what we can and should (and should not) do with our resources of time, energy and money, life becomes lighter. Burdens lift. The struggle lessens in intensity.

We come into this world with nothing; we take nothing out with us when we go. Why oh why do we spend so much life effort stacking up stuff? 'Trappings', they are called and well named they are! I suspect we accumulate stuff because we live in the senses, mind and reason only. We take on board what others and the society at large say we 'ought' to. We think and do many things without being aware of why!

One of the great aspects of reaching the age of retirement is that we are able do less, and able to do *with* less. There are fewer things we have to do, we have more time to be the way we enjoy being. Why wait until we're almost too old and feeble to enjoy life? Why not choose a small home or bus or caravan or boat? Choose less, anyway.

Apart from the burden on ourselves, this beautiful planet simply cannot afford the lifestyles we are demanding of it. It's been said before that we would need many more earths to provide all this earth's inhabitants with the standard of living enjoyed by most in the western nations. The fact is, there's plenty of what all the people of the earth need, but there's less of what a tiny portion of them (we of the Western way) want. As I mentioned earlier, wanting is the problem. In the 'good old days (tongue in cheek)', when we had far less than we have and expect now, there seemed to be more acceptance and appreciation of what we had.

Extras weren't on offer, so we didn't desire them. We were better off without the seduction of goods.

However, even if it's a little more difficult these days to choose less, we still have the same ability to choose what people of days gone by had. And we still have the same 'will'. Our difficulty seems to be to exercise our will in a simple and appropriate direction. Our difficulty seems to be to make choices that are more conducive to living rather than existing, and sustaining the life of the planet for future generations

Uncommon sense

- Realise that planet earth is finite and cannot provide all that we want. It can, however, provide all that all people need. (if we're aware and willing to share. More on that later.)

- Choose less rather than more. Choose the lower place rather than the higher one.

- Choose simple rather than complex. It'll mean you can work less 'for the man'.

- Be aware of your footprint on the planet and exercise your will (that lives in the spirit) and make it smaller (your footprint, that is!)

- Build or buy a smaller place to live. The kids don't need a bedroom and a TV each. Bunks or sleeping mats were fine for generations. Still are for the majority of earth's inhabitants. In fact, luxury for millions currently! But we're not advocating being austere. Just more moderate and sensible

- Rather than a crippling mortgage with the bank, consider living in a bus, caravan or boat. (As sea levels rise, there's going to be less land and more water; boats will make increasing sense! Already do in many places.)

- Check your wardrobe and give away those clothes you hardly ever wear and certainly don't need.

- Have fun doing good things with all the extra time you'll have by choosing less stuff!

Four stages of life

Choosing to simplify often doesn't come until the last of the four stages of life we are about to discuss. But it could come earlier if our societies afforded us the opportunity of wiser, comprehensive education; education of the spiritual selves that we truly are. In the pre-modern days of India, for one example, the culture encouraged engaging with life in all its depth and at all its stages in ways appropriate to each stage. Four stages were identified: student, householder, seeker, woods-dweller. Unlike our post-modern western approach, the ancient Indian culture encouraged awareness of, and humble reverence for, our total humanity and our interaction with all that is in our physical/spiritual world.

The obvious first stage is that of *student*. The young person is schooled and trained in all the knowledge and arts necessary for a full and honouring life. This stage is one of dependence on family and the wider society for provision of the daily requirements for life – food, shelter, security, clothing, education, etc.

The second stage is that of *householder*. The young adult marries and takes on the roles associated with establishing a home, raising children, earning a livelihood, contributing to their community, and developing expertise in a chosen field of occupation.

The third stage, that of *seeker*, arrives when children are no longer dependent, the requirements to sustain life are simpler and less costly in terms of time and money, and the middle-aged adult is freer to spend time in study of religion and philosophy, the soul-arts, in reflecting, meditating, entering more deeply into their humanity and spirituality.

In the final stage of *woods-dweller*, the aging person would leave their home and spouse, renounce all material possession, detach from the physical world as far as humanly possible, and complete their seeking to become a wise person. For a decreasing few, this four-stage path is still chosen and lived. For most, though, the attachments to life are such that being a 'purist' is almost a thing of the past. And, of course, it is possible to travel the path towards wisdom in ways other than that of the ascetic. More about that soon.

Now, here we are in the West, thinking that we are so sophisticated and clever, and superior to all who have gone before. We are able to manipulate and control our environment to suit our increasing appetites for comfort and ease without a thought for the impact we are having. Look at our impressive record here in Australia, for example. The indigenous first nation people lived sustainably in harmony with the land and, relatively, with each other for sixty thousand years. In less than three hundred years, we so-assumed 'superior' beings have all but destroyed the country's eco-systems. We've drained and/or poisoned the rivers and waterways, we've cut down the forests, polluted the air and soil with our wastes. We have oppressed, dispossessed and alienated the first nation people and pushed them to the extreme margins of life. We have caused the extinction of many hundreds of species. And we have pushed ourselves *away* from our own humanity! How did this happen?

A few thoughts on the so-called 'sophistication' of us modern men – mostly men – for the men make all the big decisions without reference to the wisdom and nurture of the *anima* – the feminine principle – both internally and externally. Sorry, boys, but we tend to stuff things up much of the time.

First, in our *student* phase of life, we study predominantly only with the intellect and the body. We reverence the activity of the mind and body above all else, extolling the dubious virtue of sport. In fact, the mind and the body have become our religions. The clever, the beautiful, the physically powerful, the skilful are our gods. Indeed, our education system effectively denies the existence of anything beyond the mind and the body. The mystery of the spirit is dismissed, because it can't be plumbed and known by the mind and the body. The result is stunted, immature, ineffectual human beings constantly in conflict of one sort or another both within and between themselves.

Then, without completing our student phase, we become *householders* – phase two. But because we haven't learned all of the student basics of our humanity, our householder phase is dysfunctional as well. If the foundation is flawed, the whole building is unsound. And because we are taught and know nothing else, householding becomes the final phase. We have 'starter houses', 'hold' them for a while and, when personal finances allow, we move on to 'hold' (we mistakenly believe, for they really hold us...) bigger houses. Then we hold holiday houses and rental houses and toys of all descriptions without any awareness of the fact that we are consuming our fragile, finite planet. Few of us wake up and realise that life is not really about 'holding' stuff. Few move onto the phase of *seeking* the truth about the mystery of life by detaching ourselves from the physical-only aspects of existence. Fewer still reach any significant degree of renouncing the sensual, mental, rational, physical world in order to be *grasped by* - caught up in - the mysterious spirit reality in and through and beyond all creation.

The results are plain to see: attachment to what is transient, fearful, self-interested, self-obsessed, greedy, destructive, discontented, anxious, depressed, in dysfunctional relationships, and constantly at war of one kind or another with someone. We are in deep trouble of our own, unaware making, and the havoc we are causing is being visited upon the earth and all its inhabitants.

Uncommon sense

- Make some time to sit with yourself and listen to the deeper inner promptings. Honour and attend that inner unrest of which we are all aware at some level that is calling us all to deep union with all that we are and all that is.

- As a wise Gestaltist once told me, *'don't just do something; sit there'!*

- Realise our need to reconnect with the mysterious inner life in order for the outer life to have any meaning or value.

- Realise that we are all *religious* at essence and don't fear that. It is our normality. Rather redefine it, as I have mentioned earlier, and embrace it as the truth about us.

- As educationists we need to shelve our ignorance and pride, and realise the senses, mind and reason are inadequate faculties to connect with all that we are as human beings. We need to start seeking and teaching kids and others the awareness and skills to 'be'.

- We need to seek and teach the ancient practices of breathing awareness, meditation, observing the mind, contemplation, detaching from the thoughts and feelings that are a constant flow for all of our lives.

- We need to seek and teach the oneness of all things, the fact that we are inextricably linked to every particle of the universe.

- We need to become aware that our actions *affect* other beings.

- Find meaning in the simple, non-material aspects of life.

- Seek to own less (be owned by less), share more, be satisfied with an adequate dwelling, conserve rather than consume. It's easier and much more pleasant and manageable than slaving to accumulate what we will ultimately leave behind and, in the process, deny millions of others the basics required for a life of integrity and dignity.

Being and doing

As we deepen our awareness of what it really means to be human, we will be drawn to reflect on how we spend our lives. We will become aware of any imbalance between our inner and outer lives. How much life are we spending on *being*? How much are we spending on *doing* stuff?

Although it's a bit trite, it's probably true to say that we are more correctly called human *doings* rather than human *beings*. If we accept the validity of what's been said so far, it is possible to move from where we are - a human *doing* - to where we could more profitably and effectively be, i.e. a human *being*. And we have some challenges, because our entire society is established upon the flawed foundations of senses, mind and reason only. Politicians mouth possibly well-meant but unaware rhetoric about jobs, education, health, security, care for the people, etc. But they seem not to have a clue about the futility of these as aims in the absence of the larger vision, namely what it means to be human sharing this planet with a few billion other humans, and countless other equally valuable creatures.

I'm reminded of the story of a Caribbean fisherman lying in his hammock under the shade of a coconut palm. An American tourist walks past in his Gucci gear and says to the fisherman, *'Don't you have a job'?* The reply comes, *'Yes I do; I am a fisherman'*.

'Why aren't you out fishing, then'?

'I've caught all I need for today'.

'But if you caught some more you could buy more boats and employ some men to help you grow your fishing business.'

'Why would I do that?', said the fisherman.

'So you could take life easy', said the tourist.

'What do you think I'm doing?', said the fisherman.

We need to change our mentality from the mindless political rhetoric of 'jobs and growth', to 'livelihoods and sustainability'. There is a world of difference in terms of effort required, satisfaction with life, and impact on the planet and all other forms of life. Jobs are about earning money to buy and consume 'stuff' – even if some is essential for survival. Livelihoods are about expressing our individual and corporate creativity in ways that enhance the experience of life rather than detract from it. And in ways that make it possible to sustain life beautifully and peacefully without stress, distress, depression, despair and wholesale destruction of all that is good.

Uncommon sense

- Take some time to reflect on your life: are you content, peaceful, in harmony with life, the world and others around you? Are you too busy pedalling the great rat wheel? Do you know why? Are you expending effort for life's necessities, or for extras that you probably don't need and that are consuming the earth and possibly denying others the basics? And denying yourself life?

- Remember the thought *'don't just do something; sit there'*! A few minutes of aware breathing and being present to yourself may provide that little relief that makes the rest of the necessary struggle manageable and even beautiful.

- We mentioned earlier that life is hard. And choosing brief and regular moments of breathing and being can soften it sufficiently to change your experience to a more pleasant one in the same circumstances.

- Resist the pressures to produce more, work harder, consume more.

- Choose simple and slow over complex and fast; choose less over more; choose detachment over attachment.

Belief and its power

If our lives are about our *true* selves in community with others and the earth's countless life-forms, we need to approach life with the humility of not thinking we know too much.

I remember a wise old monk once standing up before a congregation to teach us. He started by saying, *'I may be wrong'*. Then he proceeded with his exposition and, at the end, said *'I may be wrong'*.

It's fair to say that we don't know what we don't know. Our beliefs are just that: *our* beliefs. They are not necessarily the truth, and we need the humility to hold them loosely in order not to fall into dangerous error, and not to alienate ourselves – often violently – from others and, as tragically, from our spirits.

So many of our beliefs are irrational – that is, ill-considered and inadequately and unwisely thought through. For example, we may feel that we are not worth much and say, *'no one likes me'*. Another way of expressing that may be *'everyone hates me'*. Of course, as I haven't *met* everyone, that absolute statement is rather foolish. The truth about the situation is that *I* am talking about *my beliefs that lead to my feelings* about me rather than what others *may* be thinking of me or what the truth about me *might* be.

And we not only think irrationally, we turn that into irrational *self-talk*. That can be both over-positive and tend to narcissism, and negative and tend to self-annihilation. Each is as dangerous and destructive as the other.

A good lesson here is referred to in another cliché *'what others think of me is none of my business'*. The truth is what I think about me is the important factor. And what I think about me needs to be based on rational thinking, namely what wisdom literature, historical revelation and actual experience says about me. No matter what I may *feel*, logic tells me I am a human being with all the bits every other human being has. And, notwithstanding skill and ability differences that are always present, I have a worth of '1' (one); no more, no less. That is rational thinking. And when I think rationally, my feelings line up with those thoughts and I begin to *feel* the truth about my worth. And, ironically, others are then likely to experience me as a person of worth as well and, in fact, seem to like me!

Our beliefs need to be grounded in reality. In *fact* rather than merely in personal feeling or perception. To get it right, we need to become aware of our standing in humanity and creation, and choose to think and act accordingly. Henry Ford, founder of the Ford Motor Company, said, *'if you think you can or think you can't you are right'*. Our beliefs are crucial to how we experience life and how others experience us. Let's choose to think rationally, wisely, with our spirits as well as our minds and, thus, productively.

Of course, all our beliefs about life outside ourselves come from the inner beliefs we have been talking about here. Bigotry, judgment, condemnation, criticism, false superiority, etc., all come from irrational thinking. And this causes a great majority of the suffering we experience in our world, and interactions with ourselves and one another. Irrational thinking (cutely called *'stinking thinking'*) creates arbitrary separations between peoples and nations, and spawns wars and oppressions of all kinds, denying us all of the simple joys of being in this world and in this single human family.

Irrational thinking potentially affects everyone and, thus, the organisations to which they belong. Religions are not exempt. Although a religion may claim to have the truth, often the practice falls short of the underpinning beliefs. We need to be careful what we say we believe, because it behoves us to practise just that. And often we don't.

Call to mind the tragic actions of those who called themselves Christians in the Crusades, and more recent so-called Christian nations oppressing and violating sovereign nation states. Call to mind those of us today who call ourselves Christians, who pray for the hungry but don't feed them, pray for the homeless but don't house them, pray for those in prison but don't visit them. Call to mind Islamic State, who worship the God of peace but who kill and maim and destroy indiscriminately. None of these irrational extremists has any credibility in the heart of God whom they purport to follow and serve, and who is widely accepted by most mainstream religions to be Love and Peace.

Where we see love and peace, we see God. Where we see fear, hatred, sectarianism and violence, we see the absence of God. Where we see love and peace, we see the rational, conscious action of the human spirit. Where we see fear and violence, we see the irrational, unconscious action of the ego.

If we saw correctly, we would develop beliefs that are closer to truth and that include rather than exclude others.

Borders, boundaries and arbitrary divisions of all kinds would dissolve. More on that later.

Uncommon sense

- Watch your thinking. Observe what goes on in your head. I don't mean become self-obsessed; there's already too much of that. Rather become self-observant in a dispassionate, honest, humble, rational manner. Come to an accurate assessment of yourself, neither putting yourself above nor beneath anyone else in terms of personal worth, i.e. humility.

- Feelings are not the truth; they arise in you and belong to you and are an indicator of something going on that needs looking into rationally and wisely. Don't follow them. Observe them, own them, as far as is possible understand what's under them, and then choose to act accurately and functionally.

- Realise you don't know what you don't know and you may be wrong. The world is dying for lack of humility that excludes rather than including.

- Know rationally and wisely that you have an actual worth of '1' (one). No one else is worth more and no one less. Humbly and firmly claim it and stand on it as your 'holy ground', and afford all others the same courtesy and honour.

- Study wisdom literature and tradition in order to continue growing into the best of your personal and corporate design. And practise the truths of which you become aware.

- Reflect deeply and come to realise that we belong to one family called humankind. Race, colour, creed, nation states have no place in truth. In fact, we are inextricably linked to, and one with, all that is in the universe. Each thought and action has effect.

- Be careful what we say we believe; we are responsible to live accordingly.

Psychology, Meaning and Purpose

Psychology has much of value to say about our being and doing. It also has some blind spots.

If we take the term 'psychology' to its root, we find it to mean 'knowledge of the psyche'. In Greek thought, 'psyche' meant 'nous' - the human spirit'. A second meaning is 'the mind'. Modern psychology has, unfortunately, evolved - perhaps we should say *devolved* - to mean only the study of the mind and emotions. Our cleverness has led to the arrogance of thinking we can do away with the mystery of the spirit. We have allowed ourselves to be seduced by a lower faculty, leaving us without *the* power essential for full knowledge and abundant life. The human spirit is the only faculty qualified to assume executive function of the human person.

Tragically, some psychiatry practice departs even further from the truth about us, and is guilty of what is known as *iatrogenic illness* (doctor caused illness!) working with the premise that we are nothing more than a *'bunch of chemicals that need balancing for us to be well'*.

In more than thirty years of practising psychotherapy, I have experienced in my own life and the lives of hundreds of my clients that nothing could be further from the truth. Such incomplete understanding is dangerously incompetent and arrogant. We have thrown out the baby with the bathwater. In our desire to be in control of our destiny, we have thrown away the very quality that would deliver an appropriate sense of control, i.e. control through submission to greater wisdom and authority.

As it is impossible to navigate to a certain place without knowing where our starting point is, it is impossible to become fully human if we don't know what our essence is. As we've discussed earlier, our centre is spirit that determines effective function of all our other parts. And we've discussed the need to return to our roots in order to be well.

In our modern world, we are experiencing an epidemic of anxiety, depression, despair and all that flows from that epidemic: alienation, division, exclusion, anarchy, violence, suicide, destruction of people and infrastructure. Life has become meaningless for many who are being marginalised by the systems and structures of a profane society. Wisdom says, *'without a vision, the people perish'*. Our modern societies have become visionless; meaningless. And, where there is absence of meaning, there is no purpose, no energy, no motivation for life. In denying the existence and function of spirit, we have thrown out the essence of our common humanity and, with it, meaning and purpose. Life cannot return to 'normal' whilst we operate from a faulty, abnormal foundation.

In the first school of Viennese psychotherapy – the Psychoanalysis of Freud – it was assumed that a person's primary motivation was towards *sex*. The second Viennese school – the Individual Psychology of Alfred Adler, a colleague of Freud's for a decade – believed that a person's primary motivation was towards *power* to overcome their individual difficulties. The third school of Viennese Psychotherapy was that of Viktor Frankl who believed a person's primary motivation was towards *meaning*.

Although Freud was the father and giant of psychotherapy and many of his central tenets concerning the workings of the mind and emotions remain central to good therapeutic practice today, it is arguable that Adler, Frankl and others after them stood on the shoulders of the giant and could, therefore, see further. Moreover, because Frankl had a deeper understanding and awareness of the human spirit as the central and essential quality of our humanity, it is arguable that his contribution to the field of psychotherapy was and is the greater for it. It is demonstrable that when we find meaning and purpose in our lives, we become automatically motivated, energised to move and live and create and be fully alive. There are numerous examples of a dramatic reduction in depression in a whole population involved in some kind of social or military revolution. The revolution provided a reason to live; a meaning and purpose. Without meaning, as wisdom literature attests, we languish and die before we stop breathing.

The antidote to no meaning is to *find* meaning; to make life meaningful. Teamed with meaningfulness is *mindfulness*; consciousness. Popular psychology has recently re-discovered this ancient way of being that encourages us to move beyond our mental activity and predilections, and be conscious of 'what is'. We are encouraged to focus on, and be conscious of, simply and restfully being in the present moment, with the present breath; of finding intrinsic beauty, peace, contentment and meaning in each moment. We'll deal more fully with that in a later section.

Uncommon sense

- To be true to their names and effective activity, psychology and psychotherapy need to be seen as healing of the deeper Self; our Centre – the psyche/spirit, rather than just the mind and emotions - as important as they are to our well-being.

- See life as a moment by moment, breath by breath experience to be enjoyed in the present rather than as a goal to be pursued and achieved sometime in the future – maybe!

- Find meaning in every thought, emotion and action. None of them is to be judged as greater or less than but, rather, noticed, experienced and lived fully. Of course, it is wise to reflect upon every event and make some assessment of its contribution to giving life or not. But don't analyse to death - literally! Simply observe and be with it in any given moment.

- Peace and contentment are available continuously as we cease from desiring a certain outcome, and simply choose to be with what is. After all, if it can't be avoided or changed, our options are to accept or to reject. With acceptance comes peace and contentment; with rejection comes suffering. We choose.

- If this mystery called 'life' is a gift, we are in it and we didn't choose it, surely it must have intrinsic meaning. Our task for our entire life is to accept that meaning *is* present and, therefore, is able to be found, lived and enjoyed.

- I remember reading the story of a boy who was crying because he didn't have shoes. Then he saw a boy who didn't have feet! My mum used to say 'Count your blessings'.

- A friend of mine who suffered from polio as a child was in a wheelchair as an adult. One day, a well-meaning, kindly (but unaware) woman said to her, *'Ruth (not her real name), being in a wheelchair must really colour your days'*. And Ruth said, *'Yes, and I choose the colour'!* She found meaning apart from her inability to walk. She was also a compassionate and wise friend, mentor and counsellor to many.

- Viktor Frankl tells the story of an aged patient of his who was deeply depressed because his wife of fifty years had died and he was suffering her loss. The man's depression lifted completely when Frankl said to him, *'Would you rather you had died and your wife was now suffering as you are'?* The meaning he found in his suffering was that his beloved wife was spared the pain of loss.

Non-attachment and mindfulness

As we choose to find meaning in each of our day-to-day experiences – both the desirable and the undesirable – life comes alive. If we get really good at accepting *what is*, life can even become blissful! I confess that I certainly don't live in a constant state of bliss, but I do experience such moments, and more frequently as years go by. By accepting the *what is* of any given moment, we are released from the tyranny of desired outcome; we become attached to nothing in particular.

Non-attachment, mindfulness and present moment living is possibly the most crucial awareness and skill to develop and sustain through life. This way of being human informs everything we think, say and do every day. Accepted, practised and taught by the sages through history, this way of being has, for generations, been seen to be 'Eastern religion' and discounted as somehow 'less wise' than our western cerebral ways of being. How wrong we have been and how much damage we have done as a result! In recent decades, with the dramatic increase in world travel and consequent interaction of many cultures, these so-called Eastern beliefs and practices have begun to be widely accepted and integrated into our western cultural and religious practices. The latter have been immeasurably enriched by the mixing.

Five hundred years before the birth of Jesus Christ, sages including Confucius and Siddhartha Gautama – known by his disciples as Gautama Buddha (the enlightened one) – discovered, practised, perfected (as much as we in our humanity are able to be perfect) and taught non-attachment and mindful being. To our great benefit, this ancient wisdom is now readily available to us and has found its way appropriately into mainstream religion – albeit with much opposition from the more fundamentalist practitioners of, for example, Christianity. As we investigate what mindfulness and non-attachment are and are not, we find no conflict with the central teachings of the great religions. Every major religion has a version of the 'Golden Rule' for example. Confucius framed it like this: *'Do not do to others what you would not like them to do to you'*. Jesus of Nazareth framed it in the affirmative saying *'Do to others what you would have them do to you'* (Matthew 7:12). If you care to do an internet search, you will find a similar sentiment or instruction in each of the major religions. I find it heartening that there is so much accord between major schools of thought and practice. If only we would each submit ourselves to the acceptance and practice of such a rule, the suffering in our world would cease and we would truly be 'one', the only rational, wise, love-centred, truth- honouring way of being.

What does it mean to be non-attached and live mindfully?

Perhaps it's better to put mindfulness ahead of non-attached because, to be 'attached' or 'non-attached' is first to be 'aware' of what's going on inside us and outside us at any given moment. Actually, awareness, consciousness and mindfulness are really the same phenomenon. To be aware or conscious of what's going on in and around us at any given moment means to be fully present to those events. To have nothing distracting us from full focus on the present event. Watching, noticing, observing the flow of everything occurring in the sense and the mind. *'I'm aware of some sad* feeling in me. I don't know what it's about at the moment, so I'll breathe and be with it and, when the time is right, an understanding of what's under the feeling will emerge or not, as is good for me'. Simply observe, notice, experience, own, don't analyse or change or 'fix' or do anything; observe and be with and breathe this breath. That'll do!

As we realise that we have a 'will' and discipline ourselves, as we choose to be aware in the present moment, we are practising mindfulness. We are practising being. More correctly, we're simply being. We're not thinking, judging, evaluating, criticising, interpreting, changing. We are simply 'being' and observing that state of being; we're in it; one with it. And we are one with all that we are in ourselves. That inner harmony of all parts of our inner family, if you like – thoughts, feelings, beliefs, actions, memories, past voices, etc. – is being as completely 'us' as truly as we are able to be. To live mindfully is both to be aware of and befriend each part of ourselves and acknowledge that all parts (even those with which we are not comfortable or proud) belong in this personal 'whole' that is myself. I am 'home'; I am content – peacefully accepting and embracing all of my currently – present 'content'. I am congruent. There is no conflict in me. I am aware, present to, accepting of all that is in me at this moment. I need be nowhere else. I need to achieve nothing, there is nothing to do or prove. I simply 'am' and am aware I am. I am also aware of, present to, and accepting of those external events over which I have no control.

As we attain to this mindfulness, we experience a freedom of being. We have no agenda running, no one to satisfy, emulate, impress – not even ourselves! We are not identified with or attached to any idea, philosophy, ideology, material, spirit or anything else. We are not putting any particular store or value on anything over anything else. We are flowing in the stream of life, going where it is and is taking us, and neither desiring nor rejecting anything. This is the state of being 'non-attached'. It doesn't mean we are *laissez faire* or slack or lazy. It doesn't mean we are drifting this way or that, believing in nothing, valuing nothing, attaining nothing. Rather, our being in the flow is experienced as being one with the Great Reality that is Life, Wisdom, Love, God, Spirit, Universal Truth, and a host of other names *for that which cannot be named*. Being non-attached is to be free of our ego-defences and drives, and available to Life in all its mystery and glory, sorrow and joy.

Finally, the only place we can be is here and now; in this present moment. We can't take again the breath we just breathed; we can only breathe this one. We can't love in the past or the future, we can only love right now. We can't think, feel, speak or act in the past or the future, we can only think, feel, speak and act in this present moment. Likewise we can only find God and life in this present moment. If we are rushing through something to get to another thing, we are not alive while we are rushing because our mind and heart is in the next thing to which we are rushing. If we allow ourselves to wander into the past or the future, we will miss living the moments in which we are wandering. If this becomes a habit, the chances are we will miss the majority or our entire lives. Many people do. Remember Anthony de Mello saying, '*We are born in our sleep, we marry in our sleep, we have children in our sleep, and we die in our sleep*'?

Uncommon sense

- Being aware and mindful is noticing, observing what's going on within and around us at any given moment.

- Being in the present moment is the only place it is possible to live. We can only breathe this breath and one at a time.

- To be mindfully present in each moment is to *deeply experience* life as it is unfolding.

- To choose to accept gratefully *what is* without judgment, evaluation, analysis, or desiring changes is to be non-attached, free and even blissful.

- To be non-attached is to be fully alive in the flow of the life-giving Spirit.

- Allowing the mind to wander into the past or the future is to be asleep or, worse still, dead before we stop breathing.

Part Two:

Relating to ourselves and others

Harmony

Mindfulness and non-attachment have a great deal to do with being in harmony.

Is it possible to achieve harmony in this life? There are two answers – yes and no. As we've discussed throughout this book, the 'yes' is the internal experience; the 'no' *may be* the external experience. I say *may be* because, if there is an awareness of their spirit, a willingness by all parties to put harmony above personal ego-need to be 'right' or in control will result in making harmony possible *between* parties as well as within them.

Internal harmony is *assured* as we choose to live from our Centre – our spirit. We are responsible for creating our own experience of peace and well-being within. It may be that, as we maintain Presence by living from our Centre, that state may have an effect on those around us. It may cause them to experience something of what we are experiencing, and they may be prompted to enter into that same depth within their own psyches. The good news is that we can experience personal harmony. The bad news is that we cannot effect it in anyone or anything outside ourselves. We can only influence external harmony by maintaining our personal internal harmonious presence to what is.

As we've mentioned many times, the ego always wants what it wants and always wants more. If the ego wants harmony, its methods will always be the use of manipulation or coercion because it knows no other way of being.

Look at the efforts to Christianise the so-called heathen world throughout history. Look at the efforts – tragically still current – to 'democratise' the so-called 'barbaric totalitarian cultures of the world' – ironically via the barbaric and totalitarian methods of military action! Look at the efforts of all fundamentalist religions to force their beliefs on the world. Look at the fervour and violating efforts of corporatism *(the illegitimate ascription of the role of 'citizen' to the powerful, controlling corporate structure and function)* to serve its purposes to the detriment of the majority of the world's people. These examples demonstrate the action of ego. Total unawareness, use of the same methods they deplore, seeing themselves as right and the others as wrong. And the results are the world we have of boundaries, borders, nation states, haves and have-nots, religious and heathen, good and evil, etc. Only by becoming aware of our true essence – which is love – and submitting the ego to the appropriate executive of the spirit will there ever be harmony in our external world. While we are waiting, hoping and praying, we are each able to become Presence and experience internal harmony. That is our natural state and the birthright we have dismissed.

Uncommon sense

- Don't expect harmony outside yourself; it may never be experienced. Others have free will and may not act in concert with your seeking harmony. Each of us operates to some extent from ego, and that puts us at odds with everything outside ourselves.

- Know that guaranteed harmony is available within yourself. Seek it beyond the mind - beyond ego – in the depths of your spirit, and choose it!

- Internal harmony is unassailable; it is yours to create and to sustain.

- From your Centre, work for external harmony also, and realise that your Presence is the only influence you may 'exert'. Any other exertion will violate through manipulation, oppression, denial of the freedom of the other.

Desire or preference

Until we become aware, we generally experience harmony and well-being only when things are going the way we want them to. But that's more luck than harmony. That's having our desires satisfied. But life seldom allows that satisfaction to last. Each sensible religion and philosophy includes some version of the fact that all our suffering is caused by our desire. We want, we don't or can't have, so we experience pain of some kind. But what about the suffering caused by torture or terrorism? They, too, are caused by desire; the desire of the torturer or terrorist to exercise power or control over another.

To eliminate all suffering, all we have to do is eliminate all desire! Sounds easy but, in practice it is, perhaps, the most difficult aspect of life for us to achieve, and often takes our entire life to do so. If we get there at all! Part of the reason is that our ego – with us for the duration of life – always wants more. It is only by choosing to live from our spirits, that the pain-producing ego takes a subservient role.

One simple and manageable way to deal with the problems associated with the desire that will always be lurking is to change *desire* to *preference*. *I want* causes pain. *I'd prefer* is open to alternatives, is softer, more manageable and more realistic. *I'd prefer such and such but, if it can't be, I'll accept*, brings peace and contentment in whatever circumstance we may ever find ourselves.

Uncommon sense

- All suffering is caused by desire: we desire, we don't have, we suffer.

- To desire what we cannot ensure that we will attain produces anxiety; suffering.

- The life-long presence of the ego means that desire will always be with us. Our task is to soften the effects of *desire* by being aware of it and its folly, and exchanging it for *preference*.

- To *prefer*, accepting that we may not attain our preference, is to be free of the anxiety caused by uncertainty inherent in all desire. To prefer yet accept any outcome is to be content in all circumstances.

Forgiveness

If you're anything like me, you'd prefer that some things that happened to you had *not* happened. And you'd also prefer that some things *you* have done *hadn't* been done! We feel shame and we feel guilt. Important feelings to motivate change and to direct life. And these feelings can also be debilitating. When we've learned what they have to teach us, we need to find a way beyond them.

Archbishop Desmond Tutu wrote a book entitled *No Future Without Forgiveness*. He is an enlightened soul who understands the workings of human nature; he is aware of the *human* and of the *Being*, and knows that all our troubles are self-caused by the unsubmitted lower self – the ego. The ego is not able to forgive because it vehemently resists the notion that it might be wrong. If peoples, nations, cultures, religions, relationships, businesses, etc., are run by ego, it follows there will always be mistrust, always be fear, always be conflict, and forgiveness will be difficult if not impossible.

Desmond Tutu and all other wise people through the ages operate from the knowledge that we are spirit at our Centre, connected to a truly real, knowable yet ineffable Essence that he and many call God. And it is this God – this Truth at our Centre – that is aware of good and evil, right and wrong. And from this Centre we are able to choose fear or love, the two diametrically opposed forces within each of us, responsible for the damage we do to ourselves, one another and to our world. The healing of that damage is the attitude and associated actions of forgiveness.

But what is this thing called forgiveness? Why is it necessary? Who is involved and how? The short answer to the first question may be stated something like *bringing release and the possibility of release to all involved in a hurtful event.* Forgiveness is only necessary if you want to experience a full, free, contented, peaceful life untroubled by anything or anyone. As for who is involved, the answer is me and others. Because I am human, I make errors of judgment which lead to attitudes and actions that hurt myself. I also hurt others. And, because others are human also, they hurt me. Our behaviours have separated us from one another. Importantly – and more insidiously – our behaviours have caused a separation *within* ourselves. We are aware of an uncomfortable inner conflict. The spirit is in conflict with the ego. There's a sense of being stuck, embarrassed, ashamed, exposed and vulnerable; out of balance. Something needs to be done to put things right within me.

For a while we will deny, rationalise, blame someone or something, excuse ourselves and make myriad other attempts to soothe the hurting ego. But nothing helps until we surrender to the knowing spirit, accept the truth of the situation, acknowledge our part in it, and let it all go. It is the spirit alone that enables this letting go. And, first, we must let ourselves go; let ourselves off the hook; forgive ourselves. No-one is perfect. No-one can be. We don't have to be anyway. We all make mistakes. That's normal, human, ok, so long as we don't allow the bruised ego to prevent us from admitting the faults, owning up to our failures, doing what we can to put things right, and then even laughing about our normal, human folly!

If we've done something morally or legally wrong, we are *actually* guilty. And the spirit (of truth) within us enables us to feel it. We should feel shame as well. Those feelings are inherent in our design to signal something is wrong and needs to be sorted. But those feelings are not to be allowed to dominate and inform the rest of our lives. Before we realise the reality that we are spirit at our Centre, we can allow the ego to lock us into our guilt and shame, and spoil the joy and freedom of life.

When we are immature and unaware of the spirit, and of its executive role, we tend to get ourselves stuck in issues of guilt and shame. Often, because of the same immaturity and undeveloped Self, we can feel guilt and shame even when we have actually done nothing wrong. Psychology often sees it as lack of self-esteem or self-worth. It is more correctly seen as *inaccurate self- knowledge;* we are seeing with the ego rather than with the spirit; with the illusion rather than the reality. For forgiveness to be realised both of myself and of others, I must *see* with eyes of the spirit. After whatever necessary reparation is carried out, forgiveness of self must occur for there to be life and, as Tutu says, future.

Forgiveness is, primarily, for the one forgiving. No-one who has hurt you needs your forgiveness; *you* need to offer it so *you* can be free of the suffering caused by the separation between you and the other. The one who has hurt you needs awareness of their hurtful actions, a decision to change their ways, and a return to their Centre from where they will choose to live the future. If you forgive them to their faces, that is a bonus that will enable them more easily to release themselves from the hurt they have done to you. But your offer is not essential for them to be free of their mistreatment of you. Your offer is essential for *you* to be free of that mistreatment. *'He didn't apologise, so I won't forgive him'* is a common but ridiculous statement of an unaware person.

How do you *feel* when you have been hurt and the one who hurt you hasn't apologised? Still wounded? It's unfair? Poor me? Angry? Stuck in your suffering? Well, you are causing those feelings and it is in your power to release yourself from them. If you enjoy feeling wounded, go ahead and enjoy it for as long as you like. The other person doesn't know how you feel and is unaffected by your feelings! Someone once said *not forgiving is like drinking poison and expecting the other person to die.* It is insanity! Forgive so you may be free! What the other person does is none of your concern. If they are in error, that's for them to deal with. Your job is to manage *your* emotional and spiritual life.

A great deal is said about forgiveness in a religious context. People talk about 'sinning against God and needing God's forgiveness'. As we are made in God's image, i.e. 'in the image of love', the power to forgive or not is not in some external God, but within our own, personal *God image*; within our True, divine (if you like) Self. As the awareness of 'sin' comes from an awareness of good and evil within ourselves, forgiveness of that said sin is also a function of our Selves. Jesus said, *'If you forgive the sins of another, they are forgiven; if you retain the sins of another, they are retained'* (John 20:23). By you! In you! You remain under the power of their sin you have retained! That ought to tell us where forgiveness is located and why it is essential for us. Jesus also said, *'if you do not forgive the sins of another, neither will your father who is in heaven forgive you'* (Matthew 6:14-15). And where is heaven, where is the Kingdom of God? Jesus himself said *'it is within you'* (Luke 17:21).

So, forgiveness is not an option; it is a requirement. And the purpose is that we may be forgiven, i.e. *set free – released – from the results of all hurt and wrongdoing*. Set free to be truly alive to ourselves, each other and our earth home. Forgiveness – forgiving others – is good for us! Forgiving you is good for me! Forgiving *me* is good for *you!* Forgiveness frees us from the past thereby making a future possible, because we can't live in the past and the future at the same time! Desmond Tutu was right; there is no future without forgiveness.

Two more things to say in this brief consideration are these: first, forgiveness is not an event; it is a process; it takes time – often quite a long time. It could be years, decades or the whole of your lifetime. Hopefully it is quicker than that for you. The second is that it begins with a decision of your will; your deeper *knowing* Self. Forgiveness is first an intention, then a decision, then a committed directedness towards its fulfilment for however long it takes.

I remember the story of Corrie Ten Boom, a Jewish girl who was interred with her family in a German concentration camp during the Second World War. She was horribly abused by one of the guards. By some quirk of providence, several decades later, she met that guard. He was a changed man, humbly confessing his dreadful treatment of her, and asking for her forgiveness. He held out his hand to shake hers. Even though she was a Godly woman and believed in forgiveness, her past trauma was so deep that she could not, in her own strength, take his hand. She said to God, *'I can't stretch out my hand to this man. If you will stretch it out for me, I will take his hand.* And she did, and experienced a deeper release from that terrible past suffering. Pain runs deep, and forgiveness is difficult as our ego always feels the pain and resists letting us go. But forgiving keeps us humble; keeps us aware of and living an accurate assessment of ourselves. Forgiveness remains the best gift we can give ourselves. So, do yourself and the world a favour; surrender to your Centre and forgive! Forgive and start living!

Uncommon sense

- All hurt is caused by the ego and to the ego.
- The ego cannot forgive because it must always feel 'right'; it cannot admit fault.
- Forgiveness of self is essential for there to be life and a future worth living.
- Unforgiveness keeps us locked in the pain of the past. Logically there can be no future whilst we are living in that past. Hold onto unforgiveness at your own peril!
- Forgiveness is primarily for the benefit of the one forgiving.
- You don't need the forgiveness of another in order to be free of whatever hurt you caused them.
- Forgiveness is only possible from your deepest Self (spirit).
- Forgiveness is not an event; it is a process that can take a great deal of time.
- Forgiveness is first a decision, then an act of your will – your *knowing spirit*. It is an intent you choose and commit to for as long as it takes.

Reconciliation

Forgiving yourself and all others is a healing and reconciling action. The pain of internal turmoil is released, allowing life energy to flow freely and positively again. Parts of ourselves that were previously estranged, have come home to us, and are now on the same team!

For the past several years, a number of colleagues and I have been facilitating, in several West Australian prisons, a restorative justice program called *The Sycamore Tree Project*. Originating in the U.K. some years ago, the program is based on the biblical account of Jesus meeting a guy called Zacchaeus (Luke 19:1-10). Zacchaeus was a Jewish man collecting taxes for the Roman occupiers of Israel. Of course, he was hated by his compatriots and seen as a traitor, as he not only collected taxes, he also collected 'tips' – a self-seeking 'surcharge' that went into his pocket. By ripping off his compatriots he became quite wealthy. He was a man of short stature – and short character.

When he heard that Jesus was coming to town, he climbed a sycamore tree so he could see over the crowd. When Jesus passed by under the tree, he looked up and said *'Zacchaeus, come down; I'm going to your place for lunch today'*. The crowd was amazed that a man of Jesus' reputation would have anything to do with a 'traitor' like Zac. As the story unfolded, Zac's rapacious ways were obviously uncovered, he became convicted of his ill-gotten gains and had a change of heart. It seems that rather than accusing Zac as most others had done, Jesus graciously challenged him with who he had become and led him into his True Self.

The result was that he chose to repay all those whom he had mistreated and cheated, and Jesus said, *'Today salvation has come to this household; for this man, too, is a son of Abraham'.*

The Sycamore Tree Project was so named for its historic example of graciously reaching out to the lost, the broken, the outcast, calling and challenging them, and leading them into Life; back into the family of healthy humanity. In this interaction, Zac was reconciled within himself. In the words of de Mello, he *woke up*, his darkness was recognised, acknowledged, and illuminated by the light of Truth and love. He was thereby reconciled relationally to God and, potentially, to his community. I say potentially, because many of his compatriots were hurt by him and would most probably have taken some time to let go of their hurt and anger towards Zac and realise that he had actually changed. Some, I suspect, would never have forgiven or forgotten. Such is our difficulty.

There are several important points to draw from this meeting that are relevant to our discussion of reconciliation. First, *grace,* (meaning *'unmerited favour'*) and non-judgmental challenge rather than accusation and blame are the *connectors* and powerful healers. Jesus remained in his Centre and refused to attack Zac's destructive behaviour. When the ego senses it is not being attacked, it relaxes its vigilance, softens and become open to deeper interaction with another who is experienced as being safe. That approach is essential for developing rapport with anyone – and especially with those convicted of criminal offences. Secondly, *salvation* (meaning *'preserved from being lost in sin and unreality'*) came as a result of the ego being appropriately displaced by the spirit. Thirdly, *'this man, too, is a son of Abraham'.* He belonged to the one family of humankind. As we all do. So internal reconciliation led to external reconciliation.

Sometimes, the reverse is the case. I remember a poignant true story I heard at an International Prison Fellowship Conference in Seoul, South Korea, many years ago. It was about a little girl who regularly took a flower and gave it to the Prison Superintendent who was holding and abusing her father and others as political prisoners. She was an amazingly enlightened little girl. Her loving actions, with no hint of requiring anything from the abuser, eventually broke his hard shell, he wept, hugged the little girl, asked her forgiveness and took action to have her father released. In this case, external reconciliation (her grace towards him) led to internal reconciliation (his inner transformation) which led to external reconciliation (his releasing her father and treating others in his charge with respect).

Whatever the order, both internal and external reconciliation are desirable. Internal is essential and, like forgiveness, absolutely within our control. External is highly desirable. Of course, reconciliation with those outside ourselves is often impossible. Our legal system in Western Australia is meant to be a justice system. However, in many cases, it falls a fair way short of delivering justice. For example, convicted criminals are forbidden from having contact with their victims. So, for those who have been transformed inwardly, being reconciled to those they have hurt, is not an option. Of course, the rule is designed to prevent further traumatisation of victims, and that is laudable.

But there is a significant downside. Because of this risk-averse, adversarial, punitive system we have developed and wrongly accepted as world's best practice, both perpetrator and victim suffer more difficulty and often remain in their guilt and shame, or their fear, hurt and rage. No justice in that. Much more healing needs to be provided to those who have been hurt by crime. They can't, of course, be forced to accept such healing.

In my restorative justice groups, before challenging any of the men with their crimes, I made a point of listening to how they had been hurt in their lives. For many, it was the first time anyone had bothered to hear *their* pain. At first, they were suspicious. They thought there must have been an agenda of some sort that we were running. When they realised we were genuinely interested in them as individuals of worth equal to any in fact, they relaxed their defences and told their stories. Many wept for the first time since they were infants. Their truest selves began to appear and make peace with their darker lives – their ego selves.

One particular man of about 50 years of age, a big, tough looking guy covered with tatts – I'll call him Charlie (not his real name, of course) – had been in and out of prisons since he was 13 years old. He had spent more years in than out. His profession was that of a con-man. And, when we had *his* confidence and he knew we were on his side, we laughingly told him he should try another profession because he wasn't much good at that one; he kept getting caught! I hasten to add that we always laughed *with* each other and never *at* each other. Laughing together at our individual and corporate folly is a great way to disarm the ego and allow some light to emerge. Anyway, for weeks Charlie denied that his con-man activities ever had any negative effect on anyone. As you probably well know – as

I do personally – denial is a common ego-defence for us all when we know we have done some pretty bad stuff. Then one morning, near the last of our eight sessions, Charlie said, *'I'd like to say something.* (We were immediately attentive because Charlie had said very little to this point.) *For the first time in my life, I realise that I have victims; thousands of them'!* And this big, tough man, bowed his head into his hands and wept! And light came and healing began. He became aware of the need to reconcile within himself, and began that courageous, painful process. He could no longer avoid or deny the darkness. He could no longer suppress it nor live with it. And he became aware of the separation between him and thousands of victims that needed to be bridged somehow, sometime, if at all possible.

Look at our world. We are increasingly separating ourselves from our truest selves by engaging in noise and activity of one kind or another. We bury ourselves in gadgets, toys, technology, virtual friendships, making money, looking beautiful – anything to avoid the inner angst of not being present to our Selves. The separation is accelerating. There are more laws, more restrictions, more controls by government, more fear, more 'them and us' mentality, more illusion, more borders, more of everything that is not who we really are. And the result is widespread disaffection, less of the basics for an increasingly large number of our brothers and sisters, and more of everything materially for an increasingly small number.

The only thing that *all* have less of is peace and contentment. The few have the illusion of contentment. The many have grinding poverty and hell on earth. The few holding the illusion of power and access to every benefit in this life are obligated to wake up and see what we are doing to the many.

That is inner reconciliation. That must happen before there is any chance of reconciliation with what is outside us in the world. My hope is that we wake up. My hope is that somehow, we learn and choose to look at ourselves and the mess we're making with those deeper eyes that I've been talking about throughout; eyes of the spirit and heart. Eyes that lead us to become who we really are; spiritual beings of immense and equal worth, authentic, honouring, compassionate, responsible, protective, conserving, magnificent members of the one human family.

Uncommon sense

- Reconciliation is both internal and external.
- Internal reconciliation (of all our own 'parts', enabling us to be at peace within ourselves) is *essential* and totally within our control. It begins with awareness that we are Being; we are spiritual. And to live fully and authentically, we must choose to live in and from that spiritual reality.
- External reconciliation with all that is outside ourselves is *desirable* but can't be guaranteed as it involves the willingness of others, and physical circumstances beyond our control.
- *Grace* is the primary ingredient. Jesus demonstrated and taught *'Love your enemies and do good to those who hurt you'*. (Matthew 5:44). In *The Art Of War And Peace*, Sun Su said *'If at all possible, make peace with your enemies and avoid war'*. For us, that first means make peace with

the *enemies within us* – those aspects of ourselves with which we are less than proud and comfortable. Such grace-filled action is required to convict us of our need to submit our egos to our spirit Centre. When we do, it is possible to accept all that we are and have been, i.e. be reconciled within ourselves; be at peace. That reconciliation enables us to *see correctly – to wake up* – offer the same to others, and be reconciled to our world so that we are no longer disturbed by anything in any major way. And we cease to disturb the natural, self-sustaining processes of the earth.

Integrity

As we become reconciled internally and, to the extent possible, externally, we begin living with integrity. We are no longer divided. We are congruent. What you see is what you get.

The word *integrity* carries the sense of wholeness; all parts 'integrated' - working together effectively, harmoniously. In all that we've said to this point, that means reflecting on, engaging with, committing ourselves to know, accept and 'be with' all that we are as complex, spiritual, physical, emotional, intellectual beings. Like reconciliation, integrity has an internal and an external expression. Whilst we can learn skills of respect, right behaviour, kindness, etc., none of them will be genuine, solid, sustainable, or spontaneous and automatic unless we are first at peace within ourselves. Unless we are comfortable in our own skin. Unless we are aware of, honest about, and accepting of all that we are – the pleasant and the less-than- pleasant, i.e. unless we are integrated. Only when we are internally integrated will there be any chance of genuine, stable, secure external integration with others and all that is outside ourselves. Until then, the best we will do is make a show of having integrity – of being 'together'. But, at the first serious challenge to that appearance of integrity, our immature nature – our ego – will spring into defensive action, and we will revert to compulsive, distracted absence of balance and actual control.

As we allow the spirit to provide the leadership for life, as we are aware of and comfortable with all that we are, we somehow tune in to a deeper reality. We actually come to life. We come to know what is right and good to do in each circumstance presented to us. Our ego agendas are no longer allowed to rear their ugly heads. We don't feel the need to prove anything to anyone. We are comfortable with the opinions and presentations of others whether we agree with them or not. The battle within between ego and Deepest Self is over. The ego is respectfully relegated to the lower place, and the spirit is gently, humbly and securely restored to executive function.

Everyone and everything with whom and with which we come into contact is engaged with respectfully and carefully. The inner integration spills out onto our external relationships with all that is. Somehow, easily, life works harmoniously.

Uncommon sense

- Integrity begins within ourselves. We learn to become aware and accepting of all out parts. We learn to be comfortable in our own skin – no longer destructively self-critical or divisively self- judgmental.

- We learn that the agendas run by the ego need to be subservient to the superior abilities of our spiritual self.

- In comfortably accepting all that we are, we are able to comfortably accept all that others are as well. Our inner integration spills out onto our external world of relationships and interactions, and we inherently know how to live with and treat others honourably and sustainably. *As within, so without.* Wholeness within; wholeness without.

Games

Living with integrity means we're no longer living any sense of *double* life. There are no disreputable parts hidden anywhere, no secrets, no energy wasted in keeping up appearances. We are living comfortably in the light of truth. No deception, no agendas, no manipulation, no tricks, no *games*. Well, at least, fewer games and with awareness of them and deliberate movement away from them.

Games are interesting. We all play games. Psychological ones. And these games have a purpose – albeit a destructive one. In the jargon, the purpose of the game is called a *racket*. It's a familiar outcome for which we play, one that is negative in quality and effect, and yet neither person in the transaction is consciously aware of what the hell is going on! Why would anyone play a game for a negative outcome? Because the player is unaware of the destructiveness of both the game and the outcome. The game is played *by* the ego and *for* the ego with no awareness of the spirit or True Self in the player or the identified victim of the game.

Eric Berne, MD, the creator of Transactional Analysis, discovered and detailed these games in his popular book *Games People Play*. More than three million copies and forty years later, that book is still finding popularity and positive effect in the lives of those who discover it. Rather than detail the variety of games here, it is sufficient to outline the structure of the game.

The first thing to remember is that games are played unconsciously. We're not aware of what we are doing or why. That fact means that the player is functioning according to a pattern of behaviour that is out of their awareness and, thus, control. The underlying but unconscious motivation for the game is to get to feel good about oneself through an interaction with another that causes the other to feel bad. Example. You just bought an item and are pleased with your purchase and the price you paid. You tell your 'friend' who says, *'You paid too much for it; you got a ripped off'*! Some friend! The game they played is called NIGYSOB (Now I've Got You, Son of a Bitch). It leaves them feeling 'one up' and you feeling 'one down'.

Of course, unbeknown to them, they are really not one up at all. It is their ego that has been stroked, their pride inflated, and they have moved a little further away from their best self. Bad news for them. As for you, your ego has taken a hit, you feel wounded, you feel embarrassed, humiliated and distanced from the one who just did the number on you. And because there's no awareness of what just happened, all you are left with is the bad feeling and no real idea of what to do with it. The result is distance in the relationship. You don't feel safe with this person, so intimacy with them is either compromised or impossible; no longer an option. It's lonely. You don't even feel secure within yourself. Two needy people together yet totally isolated. Tragic.

The two in the interaction are not the only ones to suffer. Everyone in their respective circles is negatively affected by the shallowness of this unconscious life in the ego. No authenticity, no sense of freedom and well-being, no sure direction. This is the process dominating our entire world of relationships. This is the process underlying government, military, partnerships, business. This is the process ripping our life apart.

Some games leave both parties feeling dispirited (literally), some leave both parties feeling up – but it's an illusory 'up'. Only the ego is lifted and, as we've said, that is always problematic, particularly in adults.

How do we deal with games we play and games that are played on us by others? Realise we all play them. Practise being present to what is happening outside and inside you. Become aware of feelings and what triggered them. Learn to recognise interactions for what they are and, in doing so, bring what is unconscious into consciousness; awareness. Then the ego is in its rightful place, i.e. subservient to the spirit who appropriately resumes the function as your executive.

As long as the ego in allowed to be in charge of you, it remains troublesome. It refuses to admit any greater power than itself and defends itself strenuously! In believing it is acting to support your life, it takes life from you.

Uncommon sense

- We all play psychological games and they have a destructive purpose and effect on all involved.
- Games are played by the ego, for the ego and with no consciousness – no awareness – of the spirit either in the player or the identified victim of the game.
- Games are unconscious. Although sometimes knowing what we're doing, we're not aware of why we're doing it. The underlying but unconscious motivation for

the game is to get to feel good about oneself through an interaction with another that causes the other to feel bad. 'One up / one down' is the aim. But it's all illusion.

- Both achieve a negative outcome because only the ego is stroked and inflated or deflated. Unless the game is recognised and called, both move further away from their Deepest Self.

- When games are being played, intimacy is compromised or impossible.

- This is the process dominating our entire world of relationships. This is the process underlying government, military, partnerships, business; the process ripping our life apart. Inauthentic existence. No integrity. Indescribable tragedy.

- How we deal with games is to become aware of our Centre and, thus, present to what is happening outside and inside us at any given moment. Such presence provides an opportunity for genuine, caring, mutually-honouring relationships.

Defending the ego

Once aware of the games we have been or are playing, and the impact of them on ourselves and each other, we are able to drop them and refuse to defend the destructive actions of the ego – the game-player.

Defence is one of our automatic reactions when we feel threatened. If the threat is real, we are wise to protect our safety. We will fight, flee or freeze. What most of us don't realise is that we also defend ourselves when unnecessary. Or, if we *do* realise that, we are not aware of why. We think it is normal. We think we are justified. We think everyone does it. And all that is true if we continue to act (and react) from our conditioned, unconscious self; our ego.

The ego always feels under threat because the ego *is* always under threat. The ego lives in fear of annihilation because, at some unconscious place in us, it knows it doesn't have adequate resources to exist securely. The upside of that is that it constantly seeks more resources. The downside is that it seeks them in the wrong places, i.e. in the thinking, feeling, reasoning of the physical conditions of the only world it knows and the one it believes to be the real one. Of course, as we discuss repeatedly here, the world the ego knows is *not* the real world; it is the illusory world of an unenlightened self. And the ego's seeking is never satisfied, so it becomes ever more desperate, evermore narrower, evermore defended and self-isolated.

Unbeknown to the poor but well-intentioned ego, it is constantly working in ways that make its task evermore difficult and, ultimately, impossible. It wants change but continues doing the same thing – and more of the same thing. That is the definition of insanity. Albert Einstein and many before him and a few since said that *'A problem cannot be solved with the same consciousness that caused it'*. The ego needs a new paradigm that will produce new and effective resources.

As this book is not a definitive exposé on anything, and many books have been written on defence mechanisms, we will not discuss them in detail here. It is sufficient for our purposes here to mention a few of the main ones that beset us all - until we wake up! I'll be surprised if you can't see yourself in what follows. I can see me! What I encourage you to do, is to *notice* your reactions as you read. Don't judge the reactions. Simply be aware of what you are thinking and feeling as you read.

I suspect you will be inclined to do one of two things: either you will resist what you are reading and want to challenge or dismiss it, or you will smile knowingly as you discover that you actually do defend yourself in ways I will describe. The former reaction is hopeful, as it means you are alive, you've been 'nudged' (perhaps uncomfortably), and are grappling with the information that may lead you to further consider your way of being – if you allow the challenge. The latter is excellent news! It means you are already awake to some extent and willing to be with the *what is* of your current self, open to the challenge, and prepared to embrace becoming more-fully 'you'!

We defend the ego with a number of strategies or mechanisms called, unsurprisingly, 'defence mechanisms'!

The discovery of the 'defence mechanism' is, possibly, the most significant contribution of Sigmund Freud, arguably the father of psychotherapy. In my psychotherapy practice over more than thirty years, I have found them an invaluable resource – both for my own personal journey towards the light, and that journey of my clients. Many people since have built on Freud's basics as he had some major holes in his understanding of the human being. First, he demonstrated that he understood little of the deeper spirit-essence of human nature. Secondly, he based his findings on a small, unrepresentative group of highly dysfunctional subjects. Thirdly, his own personal and professional lives were dysfunctional to a significant extent. Notwithstanding those negatives, he made a profound contribution to the understanding of a significant aspect of our common humanity – the fact that we are all both conscious and unconscious.

He discovered, isolated and described what he termed *ego defences* and saw them as unconscious actions needing to be made conscious in order for a person to gain an experience of mastery or control of themselves. He saw that the ego was in a state of continual anxiety, and defended itself against the dangers of the external world. He called this *reality anxiety*. He saw that the ego defended itself against the experienced threat to the *balance of power* within the person. This he called *neurotic and moral anxiety*.

Briefly, neurotic anxiety is the fear that the instincts will get out of hand and cause the person to do something for which they may be punished. Moral anxiety is the fear of the person's conscience and results in feelings of guilt when they do something contrary to their own experienced moral code. The ego developed mechanisms to 'defend' itself against these perceived threats in order for it to not be overwhelmed, overthrown or annihilated. Here they are. And they are all unconscious; we are not aware of their existence within ourselves. Rather, when they are well formed, they become our automatic reactions to various events – external or internal. Their aim is to deny or distort reality in order for us to avoid experiencing being flawed or uncomfortable. Here they are. Have fun with yourself! Be courageous and honest! And be gentle!

Repression (bottling it up; pushing it down)

We all have painful memories. Something happens to us or we do something dreadful. We feel shocked, ashamed, devastated, humiliated, wounded or some other equally painful emotional experience. If it is too painful or threatening to face or admit, we repress it - push it down; out of our conscious awareness. This action of self-preservation is initially done consciously. After a time, though – after repetitions of remembering, feeling the pain, pushing it away – the action of repressing becomes automatic; an involuntary removal. Once removed, as mentioned above, they enter into the 'pit' of our unconscious.

They are not removed. They persist, like comments on Facebook. They remain in our psyche but are lost to our consciousness and, therefore, we are unable to do anything with them. We start excluding things within the first few years of life and they affect us for the rest of our lives unless and until we 'wake up'; bring them by some means into the light of consciousness. What brings them up is usually unbearable pain. We can repress for just so long.

Some years ago, I was privileged to work with Vietnam Veterans, facilitating groups to attempt resolving Post Traumatic Stress Disorder from which so many were suffering. Many of them had been able to repress their inner demons for about thirty years. They had managed to live for that time – albeit not with any great peace or harmony. Many had used alcohol and drugs to block the pain of the military trauma. Most relationships were strained to the limit or broken altogether. And for many, the psyche couldn't push the tormenting memories out of consciousness any longer. The pain broke through and they began to face the horror of what had been necessary to push down all those years.

The deeper essence of us – the 'knower', the spirit – continues throughout life to attempt to have us look at what is unconscious so we can integrate it and become whole and well. One of the major strategies used by our spirit is that of 'dreams'. In dreaming, our unconscious presents us with images from our own unconscious and from what is known as 'the collective unconscious' (the unconsciousness of all humanity through all time). If we make space for our dreams (time, interest and education about the 'processes of the dreamer'), they will teach us what we need to face and integrate in order to function optimally in life. Carl Jung and others have written profoundly and instructively on dreams. Of course, it is always a valuable strategy to allow a trusted friend or trained professional to gently and consistently 'call' you out when they observe gaps in your presentation that indicate missing material relevant to any particular issue with which you are dealing.

Denial

Denial is a simple way of distorting feelings, thoughts and perceptions in a situation that is experienced as being traumatic or threatening in some way. It is 'closing one's eyes' to the threat that would be too painful to 'see' and accept. Because at a deeper level in our Being we know it is unacceptable to kill others in wars or other conflicts, we blind ourselves to the fact that we are doing it. If we allowed ourselves to see what we are doing, i.e. did not deny our actions, we would become insane or destroy ourselves.

One of the ways we deny is through language. Dropping a bomb or rocket is called a 'strike'. Civilian deaths and mutilations are called 'collateral damage'. Incarcerating innocent asylum seekers and protesters is called 'detention'. Holding them without charge and without any hope of processing or release date is called 'due process'. Abrogating responsibility by jailing them in a poor, neighbouring nation is called 'offshore detention' and 'border protection'.

Closer to home, you may think you're not a bad husband because you don't physically abuse your wife; you only ridicule her and convince yourself that's not damaging. Denial is alive and well in all of us as long as we remain unconscious.

Reaction formation

This is the development of conscious attitudes and behaviours designed to oppose desires that disturb us. Examples are numerous. A paedophile may present as a trustworthy friend of the family. A violent, neglectful father may be a pillar of society. A person who is aware at some level that he is violent may present as gentle. A person who is cruel may seem kind. One who is filled with hate may present as loving. Of course, if circumstances arise that increase the pressure and drive a person beyond his ability to 'mask' the underlying motivation, he will explode, and the underlying motivation will appear in all its horror and destruction.

Projection

Projection attributes to others one's own unacceptable impulses, desires and actions. An angry person is likely to say to his spouse *'you are really angry'*. A man sexually attracted to a young girl may say that *she* gave him the come-on, so he doesn't have to own and deal with his own inappropriate behaviour.

Entire nations can be caught up in projection. The US government lies about the 'existence of weapons of mass destruction' and the 'axis of evil' projected onto Iraq produced a 'green light' for the US to violate that sovereign nation militarily. The US administration projected its own *shadow* onto Iraq and attacked it – safely distant from the 'US home' of that shadow!

Displacement

Displacement is discharging one's impulses onto a 'safer' object; one that is less threatening. For example, a woman who is afraid to confront her husband's violent behaviour towards her may take her feelings of violation out on her children. A man who is intimidated by his boss or a colleague may come home and pay out on his wife or children. If you abuse me in some way and I'm too afraid to abuse you back to your face, I will find someone 'weaker' whom I can abuse. A child who is bullied at home may bully smaller children at school. I kick the dog; the dog, afraid to bite me, will bite the cat!

Rationalisation

This is a big one! This is a way to explain away our faults, failures or losses. To create 'good reasons' to explain away a bruised ego, rather than to face the truth about ourselves. 'If she hadn't screamed at me, then I wouldn't have *had to* hit her.' 'I didn't get that contract because the guy is an idiot.' 'Your honour, If that guy hadn't cut me off, I wouldn't have pulled him out of his car and punched him.' 'If you had picked up the kids toys, I wouldn't have tripped over.'

Regression

We regress when we return to an earlier behaviour. Example: when an adult is challenged (the ego is threatened), they may burst into tears or explode in rage – appropriate responses for a small child, but inappropriate for an adult.

Introjection

This is taking in and owning the standards and values of another. We can and do introject both positive and negative attitudes and behaviours. A sexually abused child may become a sexual abuser. A female child who grows up in a household in which her father is violent to her mother may seek and return to relationships with violent men. A male child growing up in that same household may become a wife-beater or a pacifist. A male child growing up in a household in which his mother is violent or abusive may seek to avoid relationships with females. Children who grow up in families in which tenderness, honour and love are present generally become similar as adults.

Sublimation

Sublimation is 'putting down' sexual or aggressive impulses by channelling those energies into socially acceptable forms of activity such as productive work, art or creativity of one sort or another, sporting prowess, philanthropy, voluntary community service, etc. In this way, unacceptable impulses are redirected and there is often the added benefit of being praised or celebrated in some way.

Identification

Identification is a way we learn appropriate and inappropriate life-roles. If we feel 'less than worthy', it is a way to enhance our sense of self by associating ourselves with others whom we perceive to be more successful or better than we feel. We may join a worthy cause, worship a movie star or some other performer, passionately support a sporting team, wear certain type of clothing, drive a certain type of car, etc., in the misguided hope that, by association, we, too, will become 'OK'.

Another aspect of identification is when we experience a feeling or thought, identify ourselves with it and, for us, it become our reality. For example, we experience a depressed feeling and, if we focus on it often enough, we identify it as ourselves and become depressed and nothing else. The reality is that we experience depressive feelings periodically throughout life and it is merely a feeling; it is not the truth about us. An hour/day/week later, we may feel elated which is also not the truth about us; it is merely a feeling, can't be trusted and shouldn't be identified with, engaged or followed. Identifying with the qualities of another person carries with it the same downside. We are not them, they are not our reality, identifying with them will identify ourselves with a phantom – an illusion – and lead us nowhere whole or good. And even somewhere very dangerous and destructive.

It often becomes 'over-identification' in which our ideas and beliefs become who we think we are. We steal, kill and destroy for them. We wage wars for them. We put our beliefs above our common humanity and do all sorts of evil in their name. Look at the Crusades of history. Look at the person to person insult that began the First World War. Look at the Pogroms of Eastern Europe. Look at the Jihads of our present time. Look at what we do to protect 'our rights', 'our freedom', our borders', our personal finances and investments'.

In order for ego-identifications to be recognised and eliminated, it is crucial to identify with the truth about us; with the Spirit essence that empowers us to become our True Selves.

Compensation

If a person feels inferior in some way, they may be driven to develop skills or abilities in some other pursuit that gives them a sense that they are ok. For example, if a child feels unloved or ignored, they may become naughty, witty or skilled in order to be noticed, significant, and feel that they fit in and have a place in life. That was me until I woke up!

A person who feels intellectually inferior may work out at the gym and build a muscular body. S/he may be driven to develop a specialty in some area of knowledge or activity. Some of the greatest comedians, medical specialists, scientists, artists, musicians, carers began life feeling unsure of their worth as human beings. Many of them live their entire lives without being able to eliminate that insecurity. We may owe many of the great contributions to human life to the reality of compensation. But a better way of contributing to life is to recognise the reality of unconscious ego, and transfer focus and control to the working of the True Self from whom comes uncompromised value.

Ritual and undoing

If a person feels guilty or ashamed of some *perceived* wrong they may have committed, they may develop rituals to attempt to make up for that wrong. For example, an absent or unloving parent may shower their children with material gifts. A person who feels unworthy, evil, or dirty may design for themselves 'penance' or an attempted 'correction' such as excessive serving, tidying, cleaning, hand-washing, etc. These rituals may even become pathological and express themselves as an obsessive / compulsive disorder from which it may be extremely difficult or even impossible to recover. The behaviour is driven by an inner force outside of consciousness. 'Talking through' such behaviour is unproductive – even counterproductive – unless awareness of the spiritual nature of our common humanity is brought into consideration and play by some means.

The key to dealing with defence mechanisms is *awareness*. They are all unconscious and, to be dealt with, must first be brought into consciousness. It is not possible to have any effect on or control over impulses, beliefs or actions of which we are not aware. Have you ever said to a close friend, '*You seem to be quite angry about this*', to which they *angrily* reply, 'I AM NOT ANGRY'!? If we are honest with ourselves, we have all had similar reactions and almost certainly always will to some extent. What we *are* able to do is develop awareness of our unconscious impulses and actions and, thus, develop some control over them — perhaps, and hopefully, to the point of eliminating them from our persons. As mentioned throughout this book, THE way to do that is to entertain the possibility and, so, realise the truth that we are *not* our impulses which all arise in the conditioned self/ego. Rather, we are actually mysterious Being itself – spirit - which, when increasingly realised, results in an experience of full and productive life, and growing peace and contentment with all that is in any given present moment. Recognising and returning to that true centre is the only movement that will end the fear, aggression and wholesale violent destruction characterising the operation of human beings throughout the world.

Uncommon sense

- As we are each going to die someday – and that has to become acceptable if we are to live fully and freely – we need also to accept that we all have impulses and behaviours that are less than our full humanity. That is normal, ok, 'what is', and admitting it will not kill us prematurely!

- Spend some time each day – it could be seconds, minutes or an hour or so – consciously practising becoming *aware* of your inner thoughts, feelings, motivations, impulses. Don't judge or condemn them. Simply notice them, accept them as 'what is' for the present, and allow them to 'be'. The more we relax and accept the erstwhile 'unacceptable', the more they will weaken their hold on us and the more we will sense being well – peaceful, content, present to our Being. Eliminating them diminishes us. Retaining, integrating and accommodating them keeps us full, complex, interesting, rich, buoyant and content.

- Realise that we are both conditioned self / ego *and* True Being / spirit.

- Realise that our ego is attempting to keep us safe from perceived dangers in the world and within our own selves. It is trying to be a friend – an unconscious, well-meaning but often unhelpful friend! Thank it and tell it you no longer need it to be in control of your life.

- Consider and develop awareness of the ego defences that you use. If you're in doubt, ask your closest friends, spouse, children, etc. They will put you straight in no time! And they will be using ego defences too. No-one is exempt!

- Humbly accept feedback from your genuinely caring circle of relationships, accept the defences as *part of who you are* for now, and actively, consciously, pursue deep communion with your spirit – the only place where life in all its fullness is to be experienced.

- Together with courageous self-observation (not self-obsession), be kind to yourself. To be an enemy to yourself (critical, judgmental, punishing) will only serve to strengthen ego defences and take you further from your Truth.

Being Individual and Community

The better we become at recognising and integrating the ways we defend our egos, the better we become at both authentic individuality, and authentic community membership and contribution.

In ancient and more traditional societies, greater emphasis was placed on the value of the community than that of the individual. And many cultures survived and thrived for millennia – some, like the Australian Aboriginal people, for sixty millennia. The qualities responsible for such an achievement are many, and much has already been written on this by people far more versed in this than I am. So I will restrict my consideration of this to some general and essential fundamentals.

The facts are that, as human beings, we are each a one-off, never to be repeated, unique, amazing individual. To observe the complexity of humanity as a whole, you would have to say 'wow' – even to those uniquenesses with which you may be uncomfortable. It is worth remembering that *your* uniqueness may not be all that comfortable for others! Such an awareness helps to keep us humble – or, perhaps, to *make* us humble; to live truthfully!

We are also members of a large group, one race called 'human beings'. It is an interesting term that has two parts: 'human' and 'being'. Each of these parts needs our careful consideration, as each points to a reality that, together, make up the whole of who we are. And together that determine how we live and the effect that that 'living' has on the entire world and all its inhabitants and material substance.

There are two points I wish to draw out here: first we are 'human'. It's perhaps worth noting that the root of that word is the Latin *humanus* meaning 'of man'. That term comes from 'humus' (earth, soil, low). Of further significance, I think, is that the word 'humble' has the same root. It is reasonable to suggest that to be human is also to be humble. Being humble is about the most powerful we can be. We'll talk more about that later. In our human-ness, we interact with the physical, emotional, psychological aspects of our humanity and planet – both as individuals and as members of the corporate group.

Secondly, we are 'being' and are inextricably linked to the deeper, mystical, ineffable spirit aspect of Life – again both as individuals and as members of the great community of humanity.

The way of post-modern cultures throughout the world is moving away from the focus on the community, and placing more emphasis on the value and 'rights' of the individual. The ego does that. And, of course, we are less inclined to assume the responsibilities that go with those rights. The ego does that too. The benefit of this shift has been and is to allow greater freedoms of expression and creativity, and has produced amazing developments. The downside is, however, dangerously detrimental both to the health of the individual and to the one human race - and not only to the human race, but also to all other life-forms and the very foundation of the material earth. Consider, for a moment, the impact of those individuals seeking personal profit through practices such as 'fracking' for coal-seam gas which is poisoning fresh water supplies wherever it is carried out, and even jeopardising the structural integrity of the earth's crust. Consider in this multinational, corporatist, yet individual, activity the personal greed of shareholders in such companies. Consider the multitude of profit - focused endeavours throughout the world that are acting without adequate knowledge of the effects they are having on the planet and its inhabitants. Sea level rises resulting from human-induced warming of the earth have already inundated some island nations, forcing their inhabitants to seek elsewhere to live.

Of course, we – the ones who cause their dislocation – are reluctant to accept culpability and willingly take our neighbours in to live as members of our nations! One small group of individuals reaps *illusory* – usually mere 'material' – benefits at the cost to the great majority of human and other beings. And we call this democracy! Right there is a bundle of ego defence mechanisms in action – denial, rationalisation, projection, introjection, identification, to mention a few! How good would it be if all parliamentarians woke up to the fact that they are unconsciously defending their little egos, and destroying the earth and its life forms in the process!

That brings us to the interaction of both the individual/corporate continuum, and the human/being continuum. In our rapidly decaying world, it is plain to see that when we act from the 'human only' – that conditioned self/ego mentioned variously above – we cause destruction and widespread disaffection of one from another. Disaffection also from our various living environments, and of one part of the self from the other – the ego from the spirit. Over-focus on the ego is causing over-focus on the 'rights' of the individual. The result is rapidly accelerating decline for all life. If life as we know it - or knew it - is to continue, we urgently require a return to the correct focus on our essence as 'beings' rather than as 'humans'. The former (being) is the only aspect of our being capable of carrying out the executive function of living. The latter (human) is the well-meaning destroyer of our world and the corporate (community) groups in which we exist. Unless, of course, we are able to return our human nature to its healthy origin of being 'of the earth/soil/lowliness/humility'. Then both 'human' and 'being' would again be one and the same.

In traditional cultures – which were contained in, and informed by, clear and lively spirituality – each member of the community had a specific and meaningful place of belonging in and to the group. Each had a function that served both their village/community, their personal immediate family and their own self. Resources were used as needed. No one went without the essentials for a life of dignity. All had a home without a mortgage. All had a heathy combination of being and doing, rest and recreation and purposeful, community and self-supporting endeavour. It is instructive to note that depression and anxiety were virtually unknown in those cultures.

Of course, Utopia didn't and doesn't exist. To fantasise so is illusory. And, of course, the population of the earth – and, in particular, its concentration - is now such that adequate resources for all in a given locality are simply not available. The ego-centred, individualistic, western, *economic fundamentalist, corporatists* are exacerbating that inequity dramatically wherever we go in the world. Our blindness is caused by our denial of anything greater than the ego. Our blindness *is* the unconsciousness of that ego.

That blindness is vehemently denied and such suggestion is pooh-poohed as 'out-dated childish religion', 'new age rubbish spirituality', or 'anti-establishment radicalism', etc.

Sadly for us all, the truth of the matter is that 'new age' is actually 'old age wisdom of the eternal, spirit reality' that we, in our arrogance and pride, have dismissed. As scripture says, *'But they did not listen or pay attention but, in their stubbornness, followed the imaginations of their own evil hearts'. (Jeremiah 11:8).* To be guilty of being 'anti-establishment' is, actually, high praise and ancient wisdom. A word of caution, though. Being anti-establishment does *not* mean being destructive of anyone or anything in the establishment. Nelson Mandela's great wisdom and grace, demonstrated in the dismantling of apartheid, maintained that there was room in South Africa for many nations. He lived, breathed, demonstrated and taught the Bantu (and universal) concept of *ubuntu* – deep, compassionate, equal humanity. Mandela maintained correctly that it is only possible to find our own humanity in the humanity of others.

Uncommon sense

- Celebrate your amazing, unique personhood and your diverse giftedness.
- Realise, for it to be of any worth at all, it must be expressed within the unity of the Whole; the community in which you find yourself. This could be stated as follows: 'Do whatever you want, when you want, how you want as long as in doing so you do not deny any other the same right'. It's another version of 'The Golden Rule' which every culture on earth has in

some similar form. *'Do to others as you would like them to do to you.'*

- Realise we live in an individual/community continuum and need to be aware of the times for, and requirements and interaction of, both-and.

- Realise we live in an ego/being continuum also, and ascribe executive function to the only qualified 'part' – the truest Self informed and powered by the spirit.

- Take a leaf from traditional cultures and use only the resources we *need* to sustain life of dignity for all.

- There is no Utopia. But if we acknowledge and are led by our deep inner 'being' we may all get a lot closer to a quality of life that is pleasant and meaningful for all earth's inhabitants.

- Choose to minimise interaction with the unenlightened 'economic-fundamentalist, corporatist', 'greed is good', 'growth is essential', 'more is better' mindset that both characterises and destroys much of life on planet earth.

- Realise the reality that we can only find our own, genuine humanity by living and working to ensure the humanity of others.

Deepening communication

Let's move on to some lighter, awareness and skills-based aspects of life. Because the vast majority of us seem to seek to be in relationships, let's start by looking at what makes them work or fail.

There is a plethora of very good books on human relationships. In raising this topic here, I don't intend to duplicate any of them. In my thirty-plus years practising psychotherapy, group-work and spiritual mentoring, I have studied many such books and therapies, and sat under many teachers, mentors and clinical supervisors. All of them were highly trained, professional and committed to the furthering of fullness of life and harmony within and between people. And I agree with much of what they set out and practised.

In recent decades, I have also become aware that many books on how relationships work or not are based on interaction and negotiation between two egos, rather than on deep interaction and communion within and between two spirits. It seems that there are fewer practitioners and writers who plumb the depths of humanity and bring insight to the deepest communion of relationship. My hope is that I may add something of value and depth to already sound relationships and, perhaps some light and relief to those who struggle and suffer.

Being with another person or people presumes interaction on the spiritual, physical, psychological, emotional planes. I deliberately mention 'spiritual' first, because it is of primary significance for the successful wholeness of all relationships. Whilst is it true that many relationships don't acknowledge the reality of spirit/soul/God/etc.' and *seem* to work, the fact is that we don't know what we don't know. We don't know that we may be missing out on deeper dimensions of experience in life and relating to others and to ourselves. Time and again in spiritual retreats I have experienced participants report *'I thought my relationship was as good as it gets. Then I awoke from my 'ego-sleep'* (or words to that effect) *and, experienced far more depth, contentment and communion than I imagined possible, and I realise I'm only just beginning'!* There *is* no arriving at perfection in this life. But there is coming ever closer. There is *good enough* now and there is always *more and deeper*. And, as we trust in what we don't yet know - what we haven't yet experienced - and release ourselves into the mystery in and through us all and all creation, I am confident that much more quality of meaning, living and relating will be attained with great ease. Certainly that has been my personal experience in recent years.

Relationship is between two or more human beings at any given time. Without labouring the point more than necessary, it involves the 'human' and the 'being' – hopefully together and in a process that is honouring of all parts and all persons and, thus, effective. To relate, we need to communicate. Communicate means *to be and interact together with union*. It may also mean to transmit information, although that is one of the lower forms of communication. The highest form is 'being with' another with an experience of equality, safety, contentment, harmony, even 'bliss'. Generally, such communication is in silence – both interior and exterior – silence being the deepest communion possible as it is not polluted by the distraction of thought and noise and personal agenda. Such communication arises when both are open to the spirit and are fully present. If one is open in that way and the other is not, the qualities mentioned above may still be present, as the 'present one' – the conscious one - holds a peaceful, honouring space for the other to be, however they are able to be at that time. Let's look at a few of the mechanics.

As we discussed above, there is more to communication than listening and responding. And there is more to listening and responding than mere words. Studies tell us variously that words carry about 5-7% of the communication; tone of voice carries about 45% and body-language carries the rest. Of course, there are many exceptions to that suggested break-down. We have probably all experienced communications in which tone of voice or body language transmitted the entire message. There are some practical skills we can and need to learn to be the most effective listener we can be. We can be most effective listeners if, in the words, we can hear the nuances of tone, intensity, volume, pace, emphasis, vocabulary, etc. and 'match' our verbal responses to those we are experiencing. For example, if a person is loudly expressing anger, it is a 'mismatch' and absolutely useless to say *'calm down'*.

Such a response invalidates the person's emotional state and is likely to escalate it! What is more useful – and honouring – is to say, affirmingly, something like *'You are really mad about this, aren't you'!* The speaker will experience this response as *'s/he really hears me and accepts my feelings'*. They will feel heard, validated, valued, significant and are likely to respond with *'damn right'*, and then promptly breathe out heavily, sit back in their chair and become somewhat calmer. Then they are more likely to accept your invitation to be aware of their breathing and deliberately choose to breathe a couple of slow, conscious breaths.

Using words with awareness, you have matched them, paced them and led them somewhere more helpful. Somewhat closer to their Being who is present in their conscious, aware moment-by-moment breathing. This movement will help them become more aware of – conscious of – their thoughts, words and actions, and the usefulness of the same.

One more thing to say about words before we move on is this: in the study and professional practice of counselling, psychotherapy and human communication in general, a couple of researchers, Bandler and Grinder, observed the practice of the great communicator and therapist, Virginia Satir, back in the late 1970s. By meticulously analysing her sessions with clients, they discovered that each individual uses a vocabulary indicating a preferred way of 'representing' his or her world. And Virginia seemed to tune in to these 'preferences' unconsciously (at least at first) and respond with words of the client's preference. Clients experienced her responses as 'speaking their language', so to speak. The result was an experience for the client of being deeply heard.

Bandler and Grinder formed these discoveries into a system and called it 'neuro-linguistic programming' – or NLP. You don't need to get worried about the name. The essence of this discovery is that people prefer either a visual, auditory, kinaesthetic or olfactory/gustatory (V-A-K-O/G) mode of representing their world. So Bandler and Grinder called these unconscious preferences 'representational systems'. And each system has a corresponding eye-movement and hand movement associated. Bandler and Grinder called their first book on this subject *The Structure of Magic* because it seems as if magic results when a listener tunes in to the representational system of a speaker.

Of course, advertising was quick to exploit this awareness and still uses it to manipulate you and me to buy stuff. And there are many other aspects to NLP that you may wish to research for yourself. It is sufficient for our purposes here to mention this phenomenon in regard to maximising our ability to listen deeply to another. For example, if you tune in to a speaker and they seem to be using auditory words – *sounded like… heard her loud and clear… made my ears ring… he doesn't hear me…my voice and life has faded to a whisper…* and you respond with kinesthetic words like *'what did that feel like to you… her words must have hurt you… she gave your heart a belting… he doesn't know how you feel… the power of your voice and life feels delicate and vulnerable…* you will, effectively, be speaking a foreign language to the one who is telling you her story. She will experience you as not hearing or understanding a word she is saying. If you are a counsellor, she'll soon look for another one.

It's a simple skill that can be learned by practising awareness of what's going on in and around you. What are you hearing, seeing, feeling, tasting, touching, smelling? What language are they speaking? V-A–K-O/G? In reality, people use a combination of V-A-K-O/G, but have a preference for one system that dominates their vocabulary sufficiently for it to be recognised. Tune in and use words that harmonise and you will be experienced as an excellent listener and effective helper.

In the non-verbal delivery, we need to listen for/look for facial expressions, eye contact, movement and emotion, motion and gestures of various parts of the body, posture, personal space distance, changes, etc. And if we can match and pace our body language to mirror theirs, they will experience a strong, safe 'rapport' between us. They will experience us as deeply empathic, 'with them', hearing and understanding them, and they will feel safe, validated and, thus, empowered. Examples: if the person crosses their arms, slowly and as imperceptibly as possible, cross yours. If the person leans back into the chair, after a few seconds, slowly do the same. If the person leans forward and raises their voice excitedly, you lean forward too and match the intensity of their voice when you respond. If a person turns away a little when you face them squarely, you turn aside a little until they stop turning. Then you have arrived at their 'preferred, personal space-posture' configuration.

When I first learned this stuff about forty years ago, I remember going to a party and having a long conversation with a person my age. We were standing and drinking and had to be fairly close because of the noise pollution in the room and standing room only. As I faced him directly at the start of the conversation, he turned aside a little. After a while I turned also to face him squarely again and, again, he turned aside. I waited a little while and faced him squarely again and, once more he turned aside. As this was a university class assignment we had been given, I 'diligently continued'(!!) until after about half an hour, we had turned a complete 360 degrees and he seemed none the wiser! But he did seem somewhat uncomfortable the whole time. I then 'behaved' more honourably and maintained his 'off-square' preferred-facing configuration. He became quite animated, relaxed and we talked and laughed about a range of things for a while longer. And he and I clearly enjoyed the latter part of our meeting. The message here is *be aware* of what's going on within and around you'. What are you seeing, hearing, feeling, smelling, tasting, touching, and what is the appropriate, congruent, honouring, rapport-building response? It is also useful to *break rapport* when you are in a situation that is of no value to anyone and you want to end it graciously.

Remembering that it is the 'wordless' element of the process that communicates most of any face-to-face interaction, we have agreement that *silence* is a powerful communicator. We refuse to be aware of it at our peril! A favourite saint of mine – St Francis of Assisi – is reported to have said *'I preach the Gospel at all times and, when absolutely necessary, I use words'*. He was, of course, speaking about the way to live, *to be with* people; to be *in communion,* heart to heart, as it were.

Another great saint, Mohandas Gandhi, famously said *'Be the change you want'*. If we want the deepest relationship – the deepest communion – we must first be comfortable in our own skin. We must first be One with all that we truly are, to enable us to be present to, and deeply honouring of, the 'One' we are with.

I don't do that anywhere near as well as I would like to, so I keep practising being aware of when I am present and when I allow myself to be distracted. The only task when I realise that I have gone off into my thoughts is to gently (and inwardly smiling) *return*. If the one I am with is aware, they will know when I 'leave them' and when I 'return'. If they are not aware, somewhere within themselves they will still sense a glitch of some kind without knowing what it is. The best practice to adopt when I allow myself to be distracted is to simply return to the present. A second-best practice – if it seems appropriate for the person I am with – is to verbally and gently admit that *I 'wandered' for a few seconds,* apologise as seems necessary and ask the person to repeat the bit I missed. This practice acknowledges our fallibility. Our humility; our true humanness. And it gives the other person permission to be real and fallible also. It removes the psychological and emotional distance between speaker and listener, and provides for an experience of equality and, thus, 'being deeply with' the other.

It is well known that we have two ears and one mouth. It seems we are designed to listen twice as much as we speak. Wisdom literature through the ages agrees with this: *'be quick to hear, slow to speak…,'* the Bible states *(James 1:19)*. Confucius said, *'The one who speaks doesn't know; the one who knows doesn't speak'*. The implication is obvious: to listen is to consider, reflect, learn and – hopefully – become wise. To speak about what one knows is pointless unless the one to whom we speak indicates a desire to hear. Then our speech should be governed by our awareness of feedback – verbal and non-verbal – from the other, communicating that the interaction is satisfying and meaningful. And use as few, carefully-chosen words as necessary to convey what is required.

And when we choose our words, let us become aware of our personal agenda at any given time. We all have them. Agendas. We want certain outcomes. It is our human nature, albeit our lower nature. Communication theory –

which is extremely instructive and necessary for each of us to be across if we want satisfying relationships – tells us about the following styles of communication. We all use all of these styles at one time or another. All have their place. All have their limitations. Here they are.

We can be *aggressive, passive-aggressive, submissive, assertive, and manipulative.* You will know from your personal experience that there is a power imbalance in these styles, and much has been written on them that will not be repeated here. Suffice to say that the aggressive style is a win–lose (the aggressive person 'wins'), passive-aggressive is a win-lose (the passive-aggressive person 'wins'), submissive is a lose-win (the submissive loses), assertive is a win-win (both persons 'win'). Manipulative – often subsumed in aggressive, passive-aggressive and submissive styles – is also a win-lose process; the one manipulating wins, the one being manipulated loses.

On the face of it, the assertive style is the only valid one. And that is, arguably, the most appropriate style to use. However, there are circumstances in which each of the other styles is appropriate and the only one available. In cases of emergency, the aggressive style is the most relevant: *'The building is on fire; get out now!* Aggressive.

A woman experiencing powerlessness in a relationship with a controlling man may feign sickness or headache to avoid submitting for sex. Passive-aggressive. A woman (usually a woman but not always) who has a poor sense of self-worth or is afraid of her partner may be willing to do whatever she can to please him; whatever he wants, whether she agrees or not. Submissive. When both parties are sure enough of their own worth as equals, and can firmly negotiate for their reasonable needs to be met, they are communicating assertively. Both 'win'.

The assertive style is the one to be sought if at all possible, as it validates both parties as equals. However, it is not always that both parties are aware of and/or willing to act as adults in the interaction.

Something needs to be said here about what transactional analysis talks about as 'ego-states'.

In the theory, there are Parent, Adult and Child ego states from which we can and do respond. If we communicate from the parent state, it is 'parental' – often demanding, critical, powerful: *'Clean up your room'*! Parent talking to child. Powerful to powerless.

In the adult ego state – the desired state – you may hear, in a respectful, even voice, *'I'd like your room to be cleaned up before dinner tonight please'*.

The important aim is for one or both to be able to communicate as adult (ego-states) to adult. However, if one refuses to or is unable to operate from the adult, it is crucial that the other one does; as long as one remains in the adult ego state, resolution to conflict is usually achievable. The adult ego-state arises from the awareness that we are all of equal worth and worthy of respect. It also acknowledges that respectful validation – not criticism – lubricates effective communication. If assertive communication is genuine rather than merely some 'learned technique', it comes from our deeper self that we have talked about so much in this book.

This world is full of noise. And I am adding to it – although, hopefully, with redemptive noise – noise leading to silence! The noise of nature is music to the soul if we have ears to hear. Although humankind is capable of music also, much of our noise is, merely, noise and for no significant benefit. Tune in sometime and be aware of general conversation at a party or other gathering, and you'll hear what I mean! People making noise – generally from their attached, unaware egos – each talking over each other, barely waiting for one to finish so they can say the next thing *they* want to say. That is not communication. That is not relationship. That is barely *human* and far from *Being*.

If you are uncomfortable with prolonged silence, continue practising being aware of what's going on in your mind during times of silence. You may be thinking *'Is the other person bored with me? Are they content and comfortable without words? Will they think I'm a poor communicator? Do they not like me? Am I as wise as they? Am I as intelligent, impressive, etc., as they are?*

All such thoughts are of the uncomfortable ego. The spirit has no need for such thoughts and does not entertain them. Until we are comfortable within ourselves without words – without the distraction of noise – the words we *do* use will be arbitrary and not of any great significance to relationships or to the world. It is absolutely normal for us - at least in the beginning of our 'waking up' – to be seeking distraction from the background anxiety that comes with our human existence. It's called *existential anxiety* and we'll talk more about it later.

The powerful urge is to 'escape' the anxiety, 'quieten' the endless noise in our heads – the 'security-seeking chatter' of the ego – by talking. By making external noise with our thoughts. And whilst we use words, the inner anxiety moves to the background of our conscious minds. But, when the words stop, it returns. Talking doesn't necessarily serve our primary aim of peace, security, meaning, contentment. We may go home from a lively, noisy party thinking 'what a great time of communication we had'. But, before long, the underlying anxiety will re-emerge and we'll realise that we are still where we were as far as contentment and deep connection with life and others. And that the party didn't actually *do* much for us. Even the so-called 'pagan' Seneca said, '*Often after being in the company of men I return home a lesser man*'.

Now, that is not to say that lively, noisy parties are to be avoided. Absolutely not! Playing with each other is essential for health! With awareness – with consciousness – they can be much greater fun. We can still engage in exactly the same way as before, but this time with awareness of what we're saying: why, how and the effect it is having on those listening. And the effect others are having on us! With awareness, we can *observe* the conversation while we are part of it, and adapt. If we are watching ourselves and the other, we will soon know if they've switched off or not, and we can change tack. An easy, responsible way is to say something like '*sorry, am I boring you*'? and then make whatever changes to the dynamic that seem appropriate. Such awareness and personal responsibility will make you a much more interesting, authentic and comfortable person with whom to be in conversation.

And you'll enjoy yourself much more, too. You'll be more relaxed, more present to all that's going on, more comfortable with yourself and the whole environment. And you'll be aware that you are not running any agenda on anyone else. Awareness is the key! Awareness is like magic. Your senses are alive, your heart, soul, mind and body are in tune, and all is well. You are Being! You are living in your spirit! There's no better state for us. It's our natural state.

Uncommon sense

- Seek to base your relationships on communion of spirits rather than on negotiation of egos. Still negotiate for a 'win-win' as far as possible. Then pick an option: separate yourself from the unsatisfactory situation, make whatever changes you are able to, and accept what is.

- Focus on the reality of spirit first. Thought, feeling and physical considerations will then follow appropriately.

- The concept of 'good enough' relationship needs to be acceptable. Perfection is not possible in this life. There is seldom absolutely 'right'.

- 'Being with' in silence is the deepest communication possible. Wisdom begins with silence.

- Remember words transmit about 5% of any message, tone of voice about 45%, and body language about 50%

- Investigate NLP and other practices of good communication. Learn the skills and practise the awareness of 'tuning in' to another's 'language' in order to meet them deeply and, thus, have meaningful, healing, soulful interactions.

- Be aware of your own preferred 'representational system' and what you do in communication. This will enable you to become more aware of what to look for/listen for when with others.

- Listen more than you speak.

- Be aware of the communication styles you use, and their impact on relationships: aggressive, passive-aggressive, submissive, assertive, manipulative. Each has its place and limitations. Assertive style provides a 'win-win' outcome.

- Practise being with any inner anxiety knowing that YOU are not those feelings, but are far deeper spirit-Being. Peace and contentment can be experienced within any troubles we may have – internal or external.

- Remind yourself that escape into thought, noise, words or actions is illusory. Be still and quiet. All is well.

- Be the change you want. Make an effort rather than an excuse! No-one is going to fix your life for you!

- Practise being aware at every given moment. When you realise you have wandered into some thought distraction, simply 'return' to the present and to this breath.

Triangles: the geometric traps we build

As time passes, it is normal for us mere mortals to forget some of the useful skills we have learned. It is my experience that I need to remind myself often, and deliberately practise, what I know to be helpful to myself and others. Having been married to my Jenny for more than forty years, we know each other reasonably well. Often, we know what the other is going to say next, and the temptation – and too often the practice – is to finish part of what they were about to say! (I am more guilty than Jenny!) In trying to be helpful, we are often *not* helpful! Generally it is dishonouring to speak for another if they are able to speak for themselves. It is also disempowering. In groups of interacting individuals, we set up unhelpful *triangles*.

Now a triangle has many uses. My earliest memory is early primary school where I was given one made of shiny metal, and another shiny piece of metal with which to hit the triangle at predetermined times in order to make the music. Our first band! We all seemed to enjoy playing the triangle. A little later and, again in school, triangles came at us in a variety of shapes and sizes with names like isosceles, scalene, right and equilateral, and probably some others the names of which I have long forgotten. Later still, we learnt of the uses of 'triangulation' in calculating areas and designing structures that would span great distances, etc. Triangles have many wonderful uses. The Bible says, *'a three-fold chord is not easily broken'* (Ecclesiastes 4:12), indicating another strength of the tripartite structure. And, like all good things, triangles also have their downside. And that is where they are put to uses for which they were not designed. Let me explain:

A family walked into my counselling room one day and, after the usual preliminaries of introduction and a little chat with each member to confirm their importance in the group and the process, I asked Johnnie (not his real name), a 17 year old, how he gets on with his 14 year old sister. He shot a quick look at mum who, obligingly, answered my question. But what I had wanted was to hear what Johnnie had to say on the matter. Here was the first evidence of unhelpful 'triangles' in this family: Johnnie, Ruth (not her real name) and mum (her real name)! As you probably realise, mum carried all the power. As it turned out, she was the point of reference for the whole family. And she both hated and loved the role. Hated it because everything fell to her; and loved it because she got a good deal of feeling important out of the process. But it denied Johnnie and Ruth their own personal responsibility and power as individuals. They didn't get to practise thinking, reasoning, developing choices, preferences, etc. They – and mum – were all victims of the triangle!

The problem with this sort of set up is that no one gets to speak for themselves. Mum spoke for everyone else so they didn't have to, and she was so busy considering the needs of each member of her family and how to keep the whole thing together, that she didn't know who *she* really was. She was everyone else's person and, so, didn't even get to speak for herself. What a tragedy! She wanted to be caring and helpful but, sometimes, 'helping' doesn't help. She got sick and tired (literally) of being the glue, and the others got confused and angry because they didn't get to be themselves. Rather they became pale reflections of who they thought 'she who must be deferred to' wanted them (or forced them) to be. Everyone suffers and there's no authenticity or spontaneity. No real life.

The shortest distance between two points is a straight line. That's the simplest and cleanest way of making a connection between two points. When we go round two or three legs of a triangle, we have a messy and more-than-necessarily complex journey between the two points. More than being messy and complex, circumlocuitous paths don't work well in relationships. People involved get tired, hurt, angry, confused and, generally, unhappy. They feel unheard, discounted, unimportant, fed-up, worn out and, generally, unappreciated for who they are. *'After all I do for you and this is how you treat me'*…etc. is an oft-heard lament. Usually from mothers who often seem to fall into the trap of assuming the role of 'glue' and spokesperson for the mob. It is a thankless task and, frankly, one that no one should take on – except in rare circumstances in which an individual is unable to speak for themselves for one reason or another. And, even in such circumstances, permission of the individual needs to be graciously sought and humbly carried out.

Apart from being a messy communication path, triangles have another greater evil inherent in them. They carry power and control and lack of power and control. The power and control is really an illusion of power and control, because everyone in the triangle is actually powerless. And they feel it and know it at some level without really knowing what's going on. Let me try to explain:

When one is the spokesperson, they are usually in what is known in the jargon as the 'rescuer'. Now, a rescue can't happen unless there is a 'victim'. And victims don't just appear, but are created usually by the third role in our nasty triangle. That role is known as the 'persecutor'. So there it is: Persecutor, Victim and Rescuer. The system has been known for a long time as the Karpmann Triangle after the person who identified or labelled this dynamic. Even though the persecutor may feel powerful, they are actually a weak person who needs to exercise power (or the illusion thereof) in order to feel some degree of security and significance. Although, challenge such a person with their inner sense of powerlessness, and they will vehemently deny it and call you a fool or worse. Because the process precipitating the persecutor role is not in awareness. It's unconscious. Just like the games we play. In fact, all three roles are acted out unconsciously. Only when they are brought into consciousness can something be done about them. And brought to consciousness they can be. And, for life to be functional and pleasant, *must* be! All we need is the desire to get on better with each other.

One of the main problems confronting the resolution of these triangles is that the people playing the various roles get something out of the game. There's a payoff that people get used to – even when that payoff seems negative and causes them to suffer. The devil you know seems preferable to the devil you don't (yet) know. The role may give them a sense of significance, attention, connectedness to others in the group, drama (*poor me... you bastard... I'll get you for that...*). It becomes a way of life; a way of being that may give a bizarre experience of belonging. And because people aren't aware of what's going on (it's unconscious, remember), they continue to play their roles in the triangle *ad nauseam*, getting sicker and sicker as the years go by. Triangles can drive people to substance abuse, affairs, divorce, homicide, suicide, craziness, and all manner of human dysfunction. Triangles are powerful structures.

What do we do about them? First, become aware of them. Bring them into conscious awareness. Then name them, own them and, together, eliminate them. Sound simple? It is – *and* it's difficult because it means letting go of a structure that has served us in some crazy fashion to this point and we don't know how we'd be without it or with what we could replace it. That's a scary prospect. Who would I be without it? But they have to go because, as communication paths, they are clumsy and useless. As roles to provide meaning and purpose, they are outright evil and destructive of people. The only place for a third person involved in communication between two others, is as an advocate or assistant to both parties with equanimity – and if invited.

The Bible and various other Wisdom sources (e.g. Galatians 6) state that *'Every person should carry his own load'*, and we should *'Share one another's burdens'*. What's the difference? The *load* is what is mine to carry, what I am able to carry and what, for my own good, I *need* to carry. The *burden* is the extra weight that, from time to time, life drops upon us that is too heavy to carry alone. These are the times when we assist one another with the 'over load'. But, to carry something for another that they are able to carry for themselves, we collude in making them weak. If a person is obviously drowning, they need to be rescued. If they are swimming strongly, they only need encouragement to keep going. In triangles, rescues happen – whether needed or not – and only for the negative benefit of the one doing the rescuing.

But how do we get rid of triangles? How do they get to exist in the first place? I think triangles only occur when one or more persons don't know of their actual value as a human being of worth equal to every other human being. A person who knows his or her worth lives interdependently. They are comfortable in their own skin. They feel powerful enough. They have enough power of their own, so don't need to attempt to take anyone else's. Equally, they won't allow anyone to take theirs. They refuse to be spoken for and refuse to speak for another unless, as we said earlier, there is a valid need for that. They are authentic, self-responsible, maturing, human souls living as we were designed to live. And yet, so few of us actually live like this. The lack of self-worth – and its antecedent lack of knowing who we really are – experienced by humanity is endemic.

So, the first thing to do to get rid of triangles is to know who we really are. To get to appropriately value and love the person we are. To get to relax into the easy, non-grasping sense of personal power, and of personal contentment with all that we are.

A cautionary word about the expression 'personal power'. This is a dangerous expression as it can be taken to mean a self-focused 'right' that can then be exercised oppressively if we're not aware and vigilant. If we get to become comfortable with all that we are, the idea of personal power becomes irrelevant as we already experience all we need to experience in terms of our personal integration.

We've covered this adequately earlier in our consideration of who we are as human beings.

The awareness of who we really are should bring with it awareness that communication triangles have no place in our lives. If it doesn't, we may need to be instructed about the reality of their presence and danger, in order to avoid them like the plague. Once we no longer need the roles because we are now authentic, interdependent being, they will almost always drop automatically.

A last word on the Karpmann Triangle. Some time after its creation, someone added two additional roles – effective and actually powerful ones. They are *'the Real Helper'* and *'the Real Needer'* and stand *outside* the Persecutor, Victim Rescuer triangle. These roles are self-explanatory. If a real need is identified, real help is offered and provided as required. We all have real and valid needs at times during life and can't do everything by ourselves. (Even if we could, isolating ourselves from the community of humanity is not good for us.) In these circumstances we need help. That's absolutely OK. I may need a technician to fix my washing machine, or a therapist to help me get better at relating to my wife, but I don't need someone to speak for me or take over my life. The kind of helper I need is to do a job that I can't do, and then get out of the way and let me get on with living my life.

Uncommon Sense

- Triangles are strong structures that can be used for good and evil
- In relationships, they are destructive. One person speaks and/or acts for another thereby over-burdening one and removing personal responsibility from the other.

- In the Karpmann Triangle, there are three roles: Victim, Persecutor and Rescuer. These roles are played unconsciously.

- The player of each role is actually powerless even though they may think they are powerful and play in order to feel powerful or to attempt to be helpful.

- People who play these roles ae not living from their deep, authentic, spiritual centre.

- To eliminate these destructive roles from relationships, first, know who you truly are; second, bring the roles into conscious awareness; and then with assistance as required, develop new dynamics that allow each person to learn to be responsible for themselves.

- If a person is drowning, they need to be rescued. If they are afloat and swimming, they just need encouragement to keep going.

- If a person cannot carry the burden life has put on them, help is appropriate. But each person is required to carry their own load, and is only fully human and alive when they do so.

- Understand and refuse to play the roles of Victim, Rescuer or Persecutor.

- Two other roles have been added: the Real Helper and the Real Needer. There are times throughout life when each of us needs help. But we don't need to be rescued. Determine to become a real helper when there is a real needer present, and require others to always be real helpers when you are in need.

- Real help cannot come from someone who has an unhealthy personal need to rescue or be rescued.

Being a friend

A valuable friend knows when help is needed, and knows how to offer it. That same friend also knows how to ask for help as and when needed.

Much has been written about friendship. The fact is that friends are really easy to make. Some say that a deep friendship takes years or decades to develop. I haven't found that to be true. The answer is tied up with the Golden Rule: *Do to others as you would like them to do to you.* I have found that attitudes and acts of genuine love and service to another almost always and often immediately result in a return of the same.

Of course, these attitudes and acts of genuine love arise from our spirit not from our conditioned ego. Scripture says, *'Deep calls to deep'* (Psalm 42:7). When we live and relate from our depth to the depth in another, our *deep* is calling to their *deep*. The *love* in us is calling to the *love* in the other. The *love who is me* is calling to *the love who is the other*. If the other is open to her *depth*, there is an immediate identification that connects far beyond the mind. Of course it can take years and decades to catch up on the events and experiences of our individual lives. Also to share our external and internal worlds of thought, so that we seem to know a lot about each other. But those details are not what produce a deep and genuine relationship. They are icing on the cake!

A short story might illustrate.

Over the past thirty years or so, I have been voluntarily visiting prisoners and facilitating restorative justice workshops to help them integrate their experiences and further their healing and re-socialisation into the communities from which they came. In these groups, we share our common difficulties with our lives, consider matters of depth humanity, and become friends. One dear friend who'd been in for about 20 years and whom I will call Matthew, saw me in an individual visit with another guy and came over to briefly ask me if I would visit him soon. He had some things he wanted to discuss with me. I agreed and the next day phoned Acacia Private Prison (there should be no such thing as privately-operated prisons, but that's another story…) to arrange a visit the following week. I turned up as planned, we grinned and hugged, sat down and I said, *'So, mate; what can I do for you'*? His answer was telling: he said, *'You've already done it; you came'!* How easy it is to be a friend! Say what you mean and do what you say! Time is all we have in this life. Spend as much of it as you can loving others, and friendships abound and the world is a happier place. A more human place.

Being a friend to your spiritual self is always the starting point. When I am comfortable in my own skin and know who I really am, it is possible to be comfortable with you, because I know you as part of myself. There is no separation because we are inextricable parts of the 'One'. I know you in mySelf and I know mySelf in you. It is impossible not to be friends. There is no disappointment or displeasure because there are no expectations. Spiritual teachers wisely observe that it is our expectation – our desire – that causes all our suffering.

True friendship is generous, because true friendship is powered by the true self who is *love*. How can it not be generous! It doesn't keep account of who has done what to whom. It doesn't keep track of how much it gives and how much it receives. How does that work? It works because the deepest Self – the spirit we talk so much about here – is a fountain of Love – inexhaustible. It is easily able to keep on giving without any sense of being depleted. This generosity – this selfless giving between equals – is the key to peace between individuals and nations. True friendship acknowledges that there are differences in abilities to give, and needs to receive. To some is given more than to others and, from those with more, more is expected. It is their responsibility – their obligation – and honourable, pressureless duty and privilege. Some have greater needs because, for whatever reason, they have been given less. It is their right as equals to receive what they need. When all give and receive as is their ability and need, there is harmony between people. And there is peace within and between. And it is only the spirit that doesn't keep score. The ego always does.

Uncommon sense

- Remember the Golden Rule: being a friend is doing to others what you would like them to do to you.

- Attitudes and actions of genuine love arise from the depths of your spirit. They don't keep account of what is given to whom. They don't have a concept of being 'owed'; of needing to be paid back for their giving.

- Deep friendships are not based on the surface operation of the ego, but in the depths of our heart and spirit.

They can develop quickly if both are present to and aware of themselves and, thus, each other.

- Getting to know the details of another's life takes longer and is less important than the deep connection of being with. Often in silence.
- Say what you mean. Do what you say.
- Become comfortable in your own skin – with all that you are – and you'll be comfortable for others to be with. You'll also be easily comfortable with all comers, no matter what they are like on the outside.
- Generosity is the key to peaceful relating. Generosity is powered by love.
- Give what you have. Gratefully receive what you need.

The power of thought

As we've said at various times in the foregoing, good, mature friends are aware of what's going on within and around themselves. Awareness observes, reflects and causes us to act in right ways. Inextricable from this process is our ability to *think*.

Thought has the power of life and death. Thought produces feelings, words and actions that can give life or take it. If thought remains the province of the 'thinker' only (the ego), it is likely to take life. If thought is subjected to the 'knower' (the spirit in whom the 'thinker' arises), it gives life.

Much of the thinking of unenlightened humans is irrational; there is no basis to it in fact. For example, if someone in a car behind me toots his horn, impatient to pass me, I could think *'He is a selfish pig'* and I could experience feelings of anger. My immediate thought was irrational because I know nothing of the following driver's circumstances. If I knew he was rushing his sick child to hospital, my feelings would more likely be of compassion. It is the knower inside us who needs to be allowed control of the thinker. The knower suspends judgment until facts are known. This is rational, wise thinking. This is thinking that is the result of knowing. We need our knower to ask our thinker some essential questions: *'What is the evidence for your belief'?* (he was tooting his horn) *'What else might cause him to toot his horn'?* (he might be in some sort of emergency')

Irrational beliefs can cause us to think life is awful, disastrous: I can't be happy unless things are the way I want them to be. This irrationality generates self-talk which, when repeated often as is our usual tendency, becomes our 'truth'. Where is it written that you can't stand x or y? What is the proof that you are a worthless person? What is the worst that could happen to you if your worst fears came to pass? etc. If not challenged, irrational thoughts can become obsessions, delusions, absolutes; and people can become extremely dysfunctional – neurotic, sociopathic, psychotic, psychopathic and more. If we are going to participate in self-talk – and, for as long as we live and think, it is impossible not to – let's make sure the self-talk is appropriate, i.e. based on evidence, fact, reality. The knower must be accepted by us as our deep Reality, and must be allowed to be in charge of our thinker.

As long as we live, we have an ego function that always attempts to re-take control. It is always trying to do what it believes is best for us, and so is to be acknowledged as a friend. It also needs to be gently and firmly returned to its place of servant rather than that of master. Because the ego is always active, it seems that it is a life-long task to keep it in its place. Until we are enlightened (and few ever become fully enlightened in this life), the ego will generally 'hurt' at being challenged. And mine is no exception! Some time ago, in conversation with old friends, an unresearched opinion on a political matter I had expressed was summarily corrected! (In the fervour of passionate idealism, I had often been guilty of sweeping generalisations). I realised my folly. Felt embarrassed and foolish. That is, my ego was bruised. By me.

As Irrational thinking is of the ego, it takes some work to challenge and to have changes accepted. When challenged

– by ourselves or by others – there is usually some ego-defensiveness that happens as it is reluctant to admit it was wrong. So challenge needs to be gentle and associated with adequate support. It is dangerous to remove a rotten stump from under a building until a new stump has been put in place. When the building is appropriately supported by the new stump, the old can be removed. So it is with the ego. It needs to be acknowledged and affirmed for its desire to protect us.

Generally, affirmation gives it what it needs to feel satisfied and will facilitate it voluntarily 'letting go' of its previously-held, dogmatic position. So challenge, to be effective, must be preceded by appropriate support. Too much support and no change will take place. Too much challenge and change will be strongly resisted. If challenge is overwhelming, change may take place but underlying resentment and, thus, 'split' will remain and damage the individual. And the relationship. In Scripture, support and challenge is sometimes referred to as *grace and truth*. Both are required in balance for healthy growth; healthy humanity.

When challenge to irrational beliefs is effective, a change of mind occurs. Changing our minds is both OK and essential if we are to be open to becoming fully our best Selves. There is no shame in changing your mind. In fact, it is a sign of maturity and wisdom that we are humbly open to learn, adapt and grow. *'The way of a fool is right in his own eyes: but he who listens to counsel is wise'* (Proverbs 12:15). We are able to and *need* to learn from and teach each other. If we will.

Uncommon sense

- Your thoughts have the power to give life to you or take life from you.

- If thoughts are allowed to remain in the 'Thinker' (ego), they will take life from you.

- When thoughts are subjected to the authority of the 'Knower', the spirit, they will give life.

- Much thinking is irrational; it has no basis in fact. It generally focuses on the negative because of the underlying anxiety in the ego.

- Irrational thinking needs to be challenged, i.e. 'what *evidence is there* to suggest that 'x' might occur'?

- Self-talk: we all do it, so choose to make it positive. Instead of *'What if it doesn't turn out the way I hope'?* add *'so'* – **'So** *what if it doesn't...'? I will cross that bridge when I get to it...'*

- The *bad* that we fear almost never eventuates. Mark Twain said, *'The worst experiences of my life never happened'*.

- The ego is always active. Be gentle when challenging or correcting it. Remember it is an essential part of you. You don't want to do violence to yourself! Make the ego a friend, not an enemy. It means well. It simply isn't able to *do* well as the executive of your person.

- Before challenging an irrational belief or an unwise thought, put appropriate supports in place. The ego is easily wounded and will resist challenge unless it feels supported. Too much support, no change. Too much challenge, change may occur but with resistance and resentment. *Grace* needs to come before *truth*.

Conflict and Negotiation

Although our ability to think is not our greatest ability, it is an indispensable one. Especially in potentially-volatile situations requiring the presence of cool and rational heads.

In any situation of difference or conflict, what is needed is *grace;* gentleness and genuine honour for all involved. As we have discussed, grace is a function of the spirit in the deepest place within us. As long as we live, that spirit provides the opportunity for peace if we acknowledge and allow its rightful authority to guide us.

Also as long as we live, our ego is active. And as long as our ego is active, we will be in conflict within ourselves and with one another. As long as we are aware of our spirit, we have the resources to enable us to resolve both those conflicts.

Inner conflicts are normally to do with two or more ego options from which we think we have to choose in order to resolve the conflict. Inner conflicts can also be between the ego and spirit, the ego fighting to be 'right' or to be in control. As soon as we are aware of a conflict within, we deliberately return to the present moment, call on the spirit to mediate and, ultimately, resolve the conflict.

External conflicts – between myself and someone else – need similar handling to begin with. That is, the conflict is between egos, or between one ego and its companion spirit. The spirit has no conflict because it knows it is one with the other person in the conflictual event. So, given that at least one side of the conflict is coming from ego, let's consider how to deal with that.

First, we need to remember that the ego fights to be right and in control. Telling the ego in the other person it is wrong, or trying to wrest control away, usually results in greater resistance to the challenge and strengthening of the ego's position. An argument or a standoff will ensue. We need to do several things: first, if possible, rather than sitting opposite the other person which is experienced as opposing or adversarial, sit side by side to demonstrate that 'we are on the same side'. We are together against this problem. Immediately, the emotional temperature will decrease. Next, validate the person's expressed emotions and position, invite them to tell you their story about this issue and *listen!* Listen deeply to what is being said (with words, tone, intensity, pace, etc.), and – especially – to non-verbals as well. And listen to what is *not* being said. What is being omitted from the story? When they have spoken all they need to, it may be appropriate to ask a few gentle questions if the answers are not already obvious: How are you feeling about this? What happened to create these feelings in you? When did you first notice this disturbance? What is the worst part of this issue for you? etc.

Being deeply listened to by a genuinely caring person is the greatest gift we can receive. It is necessary to maintain your presence by being aware of and in control of your breathing. It may also be appropriate to invite the other to be aware of *their* breathing and, together, breathe a few slow, gentle, conscious breaths. This will further settle the person and shift them from the unconsciousness of ego to the consciousness of Presence – of spirit. That may be all you have to do. The person may realise how they have been allowing the ego to get wound up, see the situation clearly for what it is, and know what to do to resolve it.

It needs to be said that the above precis of quality listening may take years of training to achieve. And it's training well worth undertaking, as it enables us to connect to our own deeper selves and that of others.

Often, I've found that a person won't shift from ego to their deepest Self. They doggedly maintain their stance. The essential, only and sufficient thing to do is to maintain *your* presence. Be there in your spirit and don't be drawn into the ego-pain of the one who is intransigent. The conflict may not resolve to the ego-person's satisfaction. In the ego life, there is never complete satisfaction. Nothing will ever be enough. Even if the argument is 'won' by the ego position, the 'win' is unsatisfying. The ego will never be at rest, never be content.

The other person, though – the conscious one – will not be aware of any conflict because, as we have discussed above, when we are connected with our deepest Self, we are at one with all that is and, thus, unable to be in conflict. So it is easy – and the best policy – to breathe and be present when another is ranting and raving about some trivial matter of significance only to the ego. Let nothing disturb your presence and nothing will disturb your peace. *'Nada de turbe'* says the mystic Theresa and many like her.

Uncommon sense

- All conflict is in and between egos.
- We can refuse conflict by remaining in our deepest Self.
- Spirit is not concerned with ego matters and, thus, cannot be in conflict.

- Be aware of your inner conflicts: are they vying ego options? Is the conflict between the ego and the spirit? Choose the spirit and the conflict dissolves.

- Be aware of external conflicts. They are all between your ego and the ego of another. Return to your Centre and the conflict cannot continue.

- From your Centre, choose to be on the same side as the conflicted one against the problem.

- Listen with compassion and value to the story of the conflicted one. In the quality of your non-attached, non-conflicted listening, they may hear the folly in the conflict and may resolve it themselves.

- Work to hear and express all needs and preferences, then work to achieve the most honouring outcome for all concerned.

- The greatest gift you can give another is deeply listening from your heart.

- Maintain your Presence – your consciousness – as much and as often as you are able to. You will experience no conflict within yourself. And you will be a great healing presence in the lives of all who are in conflict.

Play and Sex

Conflict and negotiation are present in all relationships if we are true to our unique selves. My wife doesn't like everything about me and I don't like everything about her. That's ok. We differ on many issues and probably always will. But that doesn't prevent us from being a solid couple. We choose to separate the troublesome issues from our abilities and desires to also be playful and sexual.

Play and sex have separate lives, and they also belong together, as sex is one of our favourite games – especially for the male of the species. And not only in humans. it seems that males of many species of creature are keener on sex than are their female partners. Perhaps that's because of the burden of carrying and nurturing the young, tasks that generally – although not exclusively – fall to the female.

Speaking about us human beings, sex is perhaps the most powerful drive. Given the choice between a good meal and sex, the average bloke would take sex! I am one of those! Probably, if it came to a choice between survival and sex, the bloke might take survival. But it would be a close call!

Much has been written by writers eminently more qualified than I about the whys and wherefores of sex, so I don't intend to display my ignorance and tire you by offering more than a few basic thoughts on the matter.

First, of course, we are hard-wired for sex for the procreation of our kind. Given the burgeoning human population, the associated stress on the environment, and our abilities to resist the kinds of natural constraints the environment places upon many other species, it may be that our hard-wiring could lead to our demise. And not only ours, but that of much life on earth. But this is not the place for that discussion.

In line with our theme of the inner and outer lives of humanity, sex is also a normal human attempt at a deeper 'connection' of some mysterious nature. We have an inbuilt drive to become *one* with all that we are, and *one* with all that is. But because we are driven primarily and powerfully - - although unconsciously – by the ego, we mistake the drive to connect *inwardly,* believing it to be a drive to connect *outwardly,* i.e. to another. And the opposite sex is, generally, the most attractive to us!

For sex to achieve its three basic functions – to procreate, pleasure and connect – it is best within the context of a familiar, committed friendship. Heterosexual monogamy seems to be the widely accepted most common context, although exceptions exist with all rules. And it also seems to be most appropriate for monogamous relationships to be long-term. It generally takes a great deal of time to become comfortable with oneself in the company of another and to become comfortable with them. And, generally, in the early stages of a friendship, relaxation, if present, is usually superficial. We pretend all is well when it is often all tension and bluff. So sex is often – at least in our early experiments – steamy, lusty, tense and serious. And play, too, is usually not as deep as it can become, as familiarity and mutual honouring grow.

Of course, as comfort and mutual knowledge and honour grow, relaxation becomes deeper, and playfulness has the opportunity to bloom. The great tragedy is that most of us remain too much driven by ego and too little by spirit. The resulting tension and ego-defence creates distance between the couple such that playfulness is not significantly developed. And sex, to be satisfying, has to be playful. If there are expectations of performance by self or partner, or of some other agenda, satisfaction is automatically and, often, fatally compromised. In the 1960s, an inspiring, middle-aged American marriage counsellor, Urban Steinmetz, wrote an excellent little book about this called *Strangers, Lovers, Friends*. Among other things, about the sex act he said words to the effect, *'The couple continues playful activities until both are satisfied'*. Not a bad definition of good sex! Between good friends, of course.

In our mis-named *sophisticated* modern world, we often become lovers (or at least sex partners... there's usually more lust than love...) before we become friends. We meet as strangers, with 'good fortune' (and 'bad' as it often turns out), we become lovers and, with better fortune, we become and remain friends. Often, that order – sex partners *before* friends – prevents us from developing a deep, honouring friendship. That is a tragedy of the modern way demonstrated by the fact that something like forty per cent of marriages end in divorce.

Why are those figures so high? Perhaps because, with sex, our powerful urges are fairly easily satisfied, and the energy required for developing deep friendship is expended. Developing more depth in friendship requires such energy and can seem to be hard work. And it is! However, without putting in the best work it is not possible to experience the best outcomes. We get what we pay for. Further to that, without struggle and suffering, we won't grow. If you tear open a cocoon of a chrysalis to 'help it out', it will die. It needs the right time in struggle to develop the strength to move successfully into the stage of mature *imago*, a butterfly or whatever.

We are no different. The strongest, most resilient, mature human beings are those who have had to struggle and suffer. In adversity, we experience the distress and despair of powerlessness. We experience what it's like to be at the bottom of the heap – to be unable to get out of our situation in our own strength. This provides an opportunity to reflect on our life and seek deeper meaning in the struggle. And to seek the internal and external resources to bring to bear on the struggle. Understanding, wisdom, compassion, gentleness, generosity of spirit, quiet strength, humble self-assurance, maturity are some of the outcomes for those who use the opportunity well.

Another possibility in the face of struggle and suffering is to give up the struggle, accept defeat (or rationalise it to save face), remain unchanged and, perhaps, embittered or cynical about life. Remain on the surface. Remain immature and undeveloped. Sadly, for them and for the world, there are many who take this second path. We see the evidence in obsessive passing time with endless low-grade TV dramas, movies, novels, magazines, small-talk, gossip, glamour. With prestige, power, mindless and rampant consumption and acquisition of material 'stuff'. With self-focus, mood altering substances (euphemistically termed 'recreational' drugs: the only thing they're *re-creating* is avoidance of life) and general self-delusion that all is well. The wise ones through the ages and across all major religions and philosophies agree much of what is termed 'life' is really illusion. The Mysterious Reality is strenuously avoided for some equally mysterious reason by so many of us.

The implication of the above for marriages is the alarming and, largely, avoidable divorce rate. We lack basic training in what it takes to relate over time – first, to our deeper Selves and, thus, appropriately – and fulfillingly – to a partner. Wisdom says, *'To focus on the flesh is death; to focus on the spirit is life and peace'* (Romans 8:6). That is not to spiritualise away the wonderful and essential physical aspects of human relating. Rather, it is to place them in a context that allows them to exist and function optimally for our pleasure and our good.

It's worth remembering this too: some decades ago, there was a popular psychotherapeutic intervention called Transactional Analysis (T.A). Whilst therapy has moved a great distance since then, T.A. holds some useful awareness for relationships and, especially, for 'playful' ones. You've almost certainly heard about the 'Parent – Adult – Child' ego states of T.A. These ego states remain in our psyches to some extent for our whole lives. And the Child ego state can be further divided into at least 3 sub-states, namely Adapted Child, Little Professor and Free Child. (Our technological, materialistic life-focus is producing too many Adapted Children and Little Professors and far too few Free Children. Our education systems are deifying information and knowledge rather than prioritising the development of authentic humanity. But that's a discussion for another time). In our discussion here, it's the Free Child in whom we are interested, because it is the Free Child who *plays!* In our adulthood, it is the Free Child who enjoys deeply satisfying sex within a deeply friendly and committed relationship over a long period of time. So the ideal order seems to be Strangers, Friends, Lovers – but I don't want to start an argument! And the best friendships are characterised by a deeply satisfying 'inner connection' as well as the normal, pleasurable and conscious and unconscious connections of egos.

A word or two on play. Someone (probably Oscar Wilde) said *'Life is too important to take seriously'*. I, for one, got that really wrong and wasted a great deal of time and incurred a great deal of angst trying to live life seriously and 'wisely' because it is 'so important'. Whilst maintaining genuine honour and care for all, it is vital that when we are young, we play. Kids play naturally – although often not so honourably. With training and providence, honour comes later. So the message is 'When you are young, play; when you are old, keep playing'! And when we play, we often laugh. And we need to remember that it's only healthy to laugh *with* people, never *at* them. The ego laughs *at* people; the spirit only ever laughs *with* them. Of course, there are times when we 'take the piss' (have a joke at someone's expense) with our close friends. That's ok as long as they know we're for them, it's all in good part and they are enjoying the joke on themselves as well. They know we are really laughing with them.

As mentioned in an earlier section, we need to maintain awareness of what's going on in and around us and look for feedback as to the effect our 'playfulness joking' may be having on another. In playing, we feed on one another, the playfulness escalates and, if the ego is allowed too much leeway, we can become unconscious again. We can overstep the line on 'fun'; people can be hurt. And we can violate our own, strongly-held preferred moral and ethical positions on the present topic being 'played with'. I have often found - especially in the company of men only – the line we overstep is the *sex* line, and we easily become more crass and inappropriate than is normal for us. It can be healthy *and not* to let the 'shadow out to play a bit'. As long as we recognise where we've allowed ourselves to go, enjoy the side-trip for what it was, and return to being guided by the internal wise one, little harm is done.

Awareness can monitor the process and either stop before the play becomes destructive, or heal any wounds immediately they become evident. In a perfect world, the latter would not be necessary. We'll never achieve that perfection.

Uncommon sense

- Sex, as our most powerful, sensual drive, is a normal human attempt at a deeper connection with that ineffable, personal and collective essence- with the *Oneness* of life and all that is.
- Sex is to procreate, to pleasure and to connect.
- To be deeply satisfying, sex has to be mutually honouring and playful – as a 'Free Child' would play – without any performance agendas.
- Strangers, friends, sex-partners/lovers: for best results, get the sequence right!
- Play when you are young. Keep playing as you mature.
- Laugh *with* others – and often.

Love and Marriage

Playfulness and sex are strongly connected with love and marriage.

What comes to mind for you by the terms 'love' and 'marriage'? I suspect there would be as many varied responses as there are respondents. And there would also be much agreement. Like most people, I suspect, I often ponder this great mystery, marvelling at the complex simplicity, the powerful call to seek and know, the ever-present yet elusive reality of love's persistent enticing. My personal, puzzling search has led me to write many songs on and around this mysterious human quest. A few words from one of them.

> *What is this thing called love, is it gift or is it giving,*
> *Is it both, is it life truly living?*
> *I believe that love lies waiting inside to be discovered*
> *Not something outside me coming from some other.*
> *Love is patient, love is good, it's not designed in Hollywood,*
> *Love delights in all that bears love.*
> *Love isn't troubled easily, it wants the best for you and me*
> *Pure truth and pure mystery,*
> *Love calls all to come…*
>
> (I Prefer My Life When I'm with You: John White, 2009)

Love is arguably the most desired, dreamt about, sung about, thought about, worried about subject on the planet. Why, we may ask? Perhaps, as wisdom tradition agrees, it is because we are created for and by and *in* love. It seems to be at the centre of our hard-wiring. Because of its mysterious, ineffable nature, love is also probably the most misunderstood subject. A mystery, by definition, cannot be *understood* in the sense of intellectual activity. But a mystery can be *known* clearly and deeply by means other than the intellect. Here we're talking again, of course, about the inner life. We're talking about consciousness, transcendence, non-attachment, spirit, sometimes referred to as *infused wisdom*. No topic in life can be discussed adequately *without reference to consciousness,* and yet we spend an inordinate amount of our lives attempting just that. Limiting ourselves to the 'mind - senses - reason' interaction with life. Such attempts will never connect us with and in love. Perhaps that's the reason why there is so much oppression, fear, aggression, inhumanity, destruction in the world of humankind. We are not functioning from our Centre which wisdom tells us is Love.

What we can say briefly about love is this. Love is a mysterious Reality containing attributes famously outlined in the great Biblical passage from Saint Paul's first letter to the Corinthian Church (1 Corinthians 13:4-8). This passage is one of the great favourites for marriage ceremonies the western-world over. It speaks of the deep, imprinted desire for such an experience from and for the beloved. *Love is patient, love is kind. It does not envy, it does not boast, it is not proud. It is not rude, it is not self-seeking, it is not easily angered, it keeps no record of wrongs. Love does not delight in evil but rejoices with the truth. It always protects, always trusts, always hopes, always perseveres. Love never fails.*

As we reflect on the above, it is obvious that these attributes have a nature that seems beyond out normal human ego capability. And they are! As love is a divine quality inherent in each of us from birth or before, so the outworking of love in our lives is necessarily the province of the inner person we talk so much about in this book. We don't see any reference in wisdom literature or tradition to 'my needs, my feelings, my desires, my agendas'. Love is not about me. Love, in fact, *is* me! I am Love. And when I am *in* me – that is, when I am present to my truest, deepest Self – love emerges in all its wonder and glory and creates connection, inclusion, contentment, harmony, peace, life, joy. In fact, there can be no life without love. There can be only the illusion of life. Here, in the truth of love-in-me and me-in-love, we can see the essence of the love/marriage partnership most clearly.

Before considering that partnership, though, perhaps we should consider what is this thing called *marriage* we are talking about. In many religious marriage ceremonies, we find the words or, at least, the sentiment, *the two shall become one flesh*. Our egos generally baulk at this, although we go along with it at the time. We don't like to think that we will lose our personal identity, power, personhood, etc. and mistakenly think that's what the words point to. Nothing could be further from the truth.

If we consider *becoming one* with another person, we are simply speaking about that deep inner union both within ourselves and, thus, with another person. Of course, if we have no awareness of an inner life and think that the self we know is all there is, there is no way a true marriage union can be effected. If love is the connector, and love is our essence, and we are not aware of that fact, we haven't got what it will take to produce and nurture and sustain a *marriage*. All we will have is a wedding, an idea of a marriage, and hopes and dreams of what it will provide for me and, maybe, for you.

For there to be a workable marriage between two people, there first needs to be a marriage *within* each of them. A marriage of all the parts of their whole person – body, mind, heart and soul. Committed couple relationships that truly become marriages that survive and deepen and thrive over time, are those built on inner marriages – whether the individuals know they have done that inner work or not. Some may realise from wisdom tradition and literature what is required and willingly choose and adhere to it. Some may simply have a *knowing-beyond-intellectual-knowing* what is required and naturally do it. They are the lucky ones. The rest of us have to work hard at it. I suspect that is the majority of us. That is certainly the case for me. And that's a comment on my resistance – defending my ego – more than it saying anything about my lovely wife. I sometimes half-jokingly say to friends, *'We've been married for more than forty years now and we're just getting the hang of it'!* A long life together requires all we've got to give. And often more! And it takes a lifetime in community with a partner and others to become who we are meant to be; we find our own humanity in the humanity of others.

It's worth saying here a bit more about how we choose our partners. To be brief, we carry within ourselves an 'ideal' companion; a dream of the one with whom I think I'll be most happy. That ideal is formulated consciously and unconsciously through childhood and adolescence and, arguably, through material from the collective unconscious of humankind. It is a combination of how we enjoyed or *did not* enjoy being with our mothers or fathers, and various other influences and inputs to us as we developed. This ideal – often more perceived than real – then becomes a filter through which we look out into the world for connections with potential partners. In our experiences through this formative period of childhood and adolescence, there are, of course, deficits. All modelling is less than perfect. We carry these imperfections within us as a sense of *lack*; a sense that something is missing and causing us to feel incomplete. And our search for a mate is a search to find what is missing and unite with that. Sexual and sensual desires are, of course, a primary factor in that completeness. As we search, we *see* in a person a *promise* of satisfying what we perceive is missing. We project onto them that unconscious need, and connect ourselves to it. Marriage to that *promise* seems to be the wise thing to do to become fulfilled.

However, as sexual and sensual fulfillment are only part of what we are unconsciously seeking, after a time the old incompleteness resurfaces and we may doubt our choice. We may become bitter, angry, depressed, desperate. We may leave our partner and connect to another and another, and still find ourselves incomplete. This disillusion may become despair which gives in to avoidance of the pain through use of substances, destructive behaviours and even the tragedy of suicide. It is only through the wisdom of realising our satisfaction will never come from outside our self, that we turn inward and find within the very thing that was missing all along. The real *me*. The *spirit-in-love*! The one in whom *completing love* resides. Then we are able to see correctly, love well, give and serve generously, live fully. As we see our true spirit-self, the eyes of the heart and soul are opened and we can, for the first time, *really see* another person! We have a sense of no longer being so needy, because we have found completeness within.

Spiritual wisdom says it like this: *'Until I see the person in front of me as myself, and myself as the person in front of me, there will be no peace in the world'* (Lao Tzu).

How can marriage work if both parties are clamouring for their rights, needs, desires, sensual pleasures, etc. to be met by the other? It can't. And that's why so many marriages never become actual marriages, and why so many tragically fail before they really get started.

Marriages generally produce children. Commonly these days, a person may be married more than once, and each relationship may include children and ex-spouses and all manner of other complexities. How do we navigate our way through all that? Navigating a path through a single marriage is complex enough! Where do we place our allegiances? Do the kids from a first marriage come after or before the new spouse/partner? What is expected or required of the new man or woman in the lives of the kids? Do your kids have greater 'rights' than mine because we have moved into their house? These and other complexities are the reason why, sadly, second marriages fail at a greater rate than first. Is there an answer to such dilemmas?

In part, at least, the answer lies in the wisdom of Lao Tzu and others. We must learn as soon as possible that we belong to and in and with every other human being on the planet as *equals* in every respect. Not more, not less. And this is not well taught in families, schools, religions, philosophies, etc. We may get the official 'intellectual' version of that truth, but it often lacks deep enough consciousness in the experience and praxis of the teacher for it to be delivered and, thus, received and embraced by the student.

In reality, often by default (because of unconsciousness), we are taught the opposite: me/my wants, needs, rights, boundaries, etc. As the corollary we are inadequately taught about our obligations to life and to others.

Of course, when we 'get' the truth about 'being one with all', there is no longer 'right' nor 'obligation'. Both concepts dissolve in the reality of non-attached, non-ego, Being in Oneness; 'Being – in – Love'! That is when we become free to live as we were destined to live, and when the vicissitudes of relationships, families and blended groups no longer cause difficulties. One of the great Hindu teachers of peace explained that he is always peaceful because *'He doesn't mind what happens'*. He has no agenda, but willingly and joyfully accepts and embraces 'what is' at any given moment of his life.

Only the marriage partner who knows who they really are, is capable of relating without agenda. Such marriage relationships are sound and true, and stand the trials and joys of time. Such marriages are, I believe, the original design. Because they work.

Uncommon Sense

- Love is the most desired, dreamt about, sung about, thought about, worried about issue in life. Why? Because, as Wisdom tradition attests, we are made for, and by and in love. Love is not about me. Love is who I am at my deepest Centre. I AM Love.

- Love is a Mysterious Reality. By definition, a mystery cannot be understood with the intellect only. But love can be known by 'inner wisdom', infused wisdom; knowing by Being, knowing through loving.

- Love is not a feeling, but a response to all life from a deep, mysterious, inner 'knowing through Being'.
- *Love is patient, love is kind. It does not envy, it does not boast, it is not proud. It is not rude, it is not self-seeking, it is not easily angered, it keeps no record of wrongs. Love does not delight in evil but rejoices with the truth. It always protects, always trusts, always hopes, always perseveres. Love never fails. (1 Corinthians 13:4-8)*
- Love connects, includes, harmonises, makes peace.
- Love comes from and creates *Oneness*.
- For marriages to truly succeed, each participant must experience an 'inner marriage'; marriage within the Self, i.e. the aspects of shadow and light, anima and animus, folly and wisdom, (so-called) positives and negatives.
- In successful marriage – as in all successful relationships – *'I must see the person in front of me as myself, and myself as the person in front of me'* (Lao Tzu).
- Love engages with and successfully navigates the complexities of life in traditional and blended family units.
- 'Being – in- Love' is who we really are at our deepest Centre. Living and relating from that Centre enables us to jointly create the most mature, meaningful and fulfilling marriages and communities.

Sex and Language as 'weapons'

But what if sex and play and love and marriage are not the nice events that are the desired ideal? What if aspects of sex, play and relationship language are used as weapons as they so often are? How does that happen and what can be done about it?

A great deal has been and is being written and talked about the toxic aspects of relationships – particularly between males and females. In feminist literature, the term 'toxic masculinity' appears referring to *immature (unconscious)* males who are abusive in one way or another to females; males who commonly use sex and language to oppress and violate; to demean, abuse and rape females. How does it happen that some males seem to think that the female exists to provide them with sexual and psychological gratification? How does a culture come to be characterised by arbitrary divisions between what is for girls and what is for boys and the diabolical implications of that for both genders?

The answer lies somewhere in inappropriate socialisation from one generation to the next. And, as we've said often in this book, it is generally the unconscious self – the troublesome ego - that does the socialising. If the spirit was recognised and given the task, the abuses suffered by females would not occur. Males would become men in the truest sense of the word, interacting with their female human counterparts as the equals they are. Regarding females with the deepest honour – indeed, *reverence*, is not inappropriate. Every human being is worthy of being revered. Every human being deserves to live in safety and be afforded the opportunity to express the fullness of their uniqueness without interference from any other human being.

At present, because relationships are run mostly by the unconscious ego, the desperate desires of that ego for power, control, superiority, sensual and sexual gratification, it has become normal for males to justify inappropriate behaviour towards females. It has become normal for males not to accept personal responsibility for their behaviours. Further, it has become normal to require the female to modify her behaviour – dress, manner, makeup, etc. – so as not to arouse bad behaviour in males! How disgusting and pathetic and *unmanly* is that? True masculinity is strong in its gentleness, self-control, and self-responsibility. Resolute and committed in its value and respect for all other beings – females and males. True masculinity gives rather than takes, serves rather than being served, nurtures rather than destroys. Toxicity has no place in masculinity. In fact, no place in humanity. And *deep* masculinity – and deep femininity for that matter – is only attained by knowing the truth about ones-self, knowing and resting securely in the spiritual reality in one's Centre, and being directed from that Centre in all of life's activities. How men are able to demean, oppress, abuse, rape, destroy females is that they haven't learned who they really are and, thus, with whom they are interacting: their own, spirit Self!

Uncommon sense

- Sex, play and relationship language can be and are often used by immature males as *weapons* to degrade, dishonour and destroy the lives of females.

- Immature males mistakenly believe females exist to provide them with sensual, sexual and psychological gratification.

- Inappropriate socialisation from one generation to the next is responsible for arbitrary divisions between *what is for girls and what is for boys.*

- Toxic males are immature and unconscious, believing their egos are who they are and, thus, behaving in ways that dishonour themselves and others.

- The ego's desperate desire for power, control, superiority, sensual/sexual gratification drives abusive behaviour.

- True masculinity is strong in its gentleness, self-control and self-responsibility.

- To be deeply masculine – truly *manly* – is to be guided from the deepest Self – the spirit that is *'giving' love.*

Support and Challenge

Strong, safe, nurturing relationships are characterised by deep Self-knowledge, and associated, balanced combination of support and challenge; grace and truth.

Training to be a therapist, an essential part of the process is to work on your own 'stuff' – your own personal growth needs. That's standard procedure for any program that's worth anything. And when you start working with clients, you must spend regular time with a clinical supervisor, who is a senior and experienced therapist who oversees your casework and helps you identify and deal with your personal issues that arise whenever you work with another person's issues.

One of my early therapists and supervisors, Ian Mackie who would have been, at the time, one of Australia's most skilful therapists, taught me much of what I have since found useful and effective. Other than the myriad listening and responding skills essential to sustaining presence and maintaining rapport with a person in trouble, I came to know the indispensable understanding and skill of balancing 'support and challenge'. And Ian taught me by allowing me to experience them. I was telling him about some pathetic little dilemma I was in and he, very graciously, said to me, *'John, I can see this is very difficult for you'*. I felt like throwing my arms around him! Here was a person who understood my pain like I had never felt understood before in my life. That simple response was support. And, because Ian put that in place at the outset, I felt I had a safe companion on the journey. I wasn't alone and didn't feel judged or scared. Ian's companionable, wise, skilful support gave me the strength I needed to endure the challenges he brought me in due time to gently and firmly push me in the direction of new decisions and behaviours that eventually got me unstuck and functional. Well, reasonably functional.

So, in all the years of training, study and learning to become a useful therapist – about 40 so far – two of the most centrally relevant and useful truths I have learned are the Siamese-twin concepts of *support* and *challenge*. And they can never be separated. To give credit where it is due, those concepts are the secular equivalent of the Biblical concepts of 'Grace and Truth' (See John 1:14).

Actually, they are two sides of the one truth really. Grace for the purpose of holding and providing safety; Truth for getting us unstuck and moving towards healing and wholeness. As we mentioned in passing in an earlier discussion, support alone doesn't achieve movement. It achieves support. Similarly, challenge on its own doesn't achieve movement either. But challenge is the part that achieves movement when appropriate support is first in place. Too much of one or the other doesn't work. Too much support leaves a person feeling listened to, empathised with, understood, valued but not really helped by all that connecting, as valuable and essential as it is.

This is a fault more common to untrained women than to men, as women tend to be naturally more compassionate and gentler in their interactions. Too much challenge and the person doesn't feel any of the abovementioned warmth, but feels pushed, feels another expectation they can't meet. They experience being further wounded and traumatised, and may withdraw into the pain not to come out again. This is the domain mostly of untrained men who want to cut to the chase, fix the problem, *'Pull your finger out and get on with it'*. Men need to learn from women and women need to learn from men. It's no accident that men and women generally are attracted to each other and somehow know (apart from sexual attraction) that they need to team up to help each become two effective functional adults.

It's crucial to get these two faces of the one gem in balance and working together. There is an order; there's a right way to implement these. If you challenge me while I'm raw and hurting, I'll close up and shut you out and me in. You have to connect with my pain first and let me experience your genuine understanding and holding love and respect for me so I'll be able and willing to entrust myself to you; so I'll risk coming out and telling you my story. Support first or you don't earn the opportunity to challenge. When we know we are valued, loved, and safe, we will endure being challenged to change.

A friend of mine told me recently that when she was a child, if she told her mother some task was *'Too hard; I can't do it!'*, her mother said, *'Try harder'*. She did and, now in her eighties, remains the very capable, competent, caring adult she became during those formative years. For her, the challenge from her mum came in combination with safe, supportive home life. She knew she was loved.

Why don't men readily open up to each other? Partly, because it's culturally not cool to talk about your emotions and inability to cope with life. Accordingly, men are emotionally far more crippled than women. To be brutalised by your mate and be told *'Don't be bloody silly… pull your finger out and get on with it… put it behind you, mate, it's over… you can't do anything about it'*, etc., is not helpful! So most men won't again risk exposing their vulnerabilities. Once burnt; twice shy. On the other hand, it's culturally normal for women to talk about their emotions and lovingly support each other through their struggles. Many have developed the awareness, the intuition and enough of the skills to be quite helpful to others even without formal training.

We men desperately need to learn these skills from our womenfolk so we can be agents of healing for our male mates. If this were globally achieved, there would be no more war or famine. And it's as simple as learning who we really are. Getting comfortable in our own skin. Learning how to love, cutting through the bullshit of 'machismo', and learning how to nurture ourselves and others. And this is not to become wimpy or a sensitive new-age guy. It's actually to become strong. True strength is gentle and gentleness is true strength.

In-depth discussion about how and what skills to develop to achieve the outcome suggested above has been amply covered in many other books. I encourage us all to seek everywhere to become as fully human men and women as we can during this short life. The place to begin, as I have often mentioned, is to know who we truly are as spiritual beings – soul people – created in and by and for 'Love'. Without that correct foundation, anything we build will be fatally compromised, and the mess we make of our earth will be unabated.

Uncommon sense

- We won't be much help to anyone if we don't realise that grace and truth, support and challenge, are essential qualities and skills to develop and implement. They belong together in the right sequence and the right balance.

- Support must be provided first so the person feels safe with you, respected and understood by you; sufficiently safe to be able to tell their story and accommodate the challenge when it comes (and come it must for movement and growth to take place).

- You'll know if you've challenged too soon. The person will recoil, their eyes will glaze over or avert, they will look uncomfortable. They may become angry or have any number of other reactions that will tell you you've broken rapport. The sharing will become superficial or stop. The person may leave your presence and not return.

- If you notice the withdrawal soon enough, you can repair rapport and continue.

- Men need to learn from women how to manage the emotional life so we can be agents of healing for our male mates.

- Machismo has no place in mature adult relationships.

- True strength is gentle, and gentleness is true strength.

How shall we live?

Support and challenge in the correct order and balance are essential for each of us as we deal with ourselves and each other. Without acquiring this awareness and achieving the associated skill, we will continue existing in conflict both within and between individuals and nations.

Our world is characterised more each day by division and conflict. We have plenty of *know how*, but little *know what*. We have lost awareness of who we are as human beings and what our priorities ought to be. In the words of E. F. Schumacher, author of *Small Is Beautiful,* there are too many of us in 'the forward stampede', and too few 'home-comers'. For life on earth to survive, we must reverse the present trend. That is not to overstate concern.

What is the *forward stampede*? It is the increasingly frantic movement of life, driving and being driven by corporatism and its associated desire to consume ever more material and experience continual emotional and physical stimulation. This is the stampede of unawareness; of human immaturity; of distraction from appropriate focus.

Why do we say that? The drive to acquire and consume material goods, services and experiences is a clear indicator of discomfort; discontent with ourselves and our life as it currently is. We feel that something is missing – something is not right – and we attempt to remedy that by input of one kind or another from outside the self.

This is an unconscious and futile attempt to dispel the unrest. And, because the input doesn't remove the discomfort, we put in more and more in the vain hope that more will solve the problem. But, of course, it doesn't, and we lock ourselves into a cycle of unrest – consume/distract – brief relief – unrest. The cycle becomes an addictive automatic pattern of behaviour, and 'me-mine-fear-greed' is the self-perpetuating outcome. This deathly cycle – this 'forward stampede' – is the lot of human beings who don't yet know who they really are. It is that which Viktor Frankl termed the *existential vacuum* – the experience of existing in a seemingly meaningless confusion and fear-filled life.

This human activity – this 'stampede' – is created and driven by an inappropriate and fatally flawed understanding of the place of economics in our world. Economics was to be the servant of social humanity, but it has become the master – and an evil, tyrannical master at that. Under the guise of democracy, the so-called 'free market' is free only to the diminishing few who own the market and its material benefits. This mind-set is promulgated and promoted until it is now accepted as an inviolable given, and allowed to increasingly weave its oppression on the majority. And we need to make no mistake: the term 'democracy' has, unfortunately, become a euphemism for corporatism – a system of self-indulgent, fear-based, greed and oppression for the benefit of a tiny minority. This minority, often called the '1%', is more accurately the 0.1%. And, even within this self-important, self-indulgent, tiny group, there is a further level of greed and oppression that allows top *male* CEO's to be rewarded with salary packages many times that of their female counterparts.

And who are the *'home-comers'*? They are the self-aware, wise and brave souls who correctly see the folly of the system assumed to be the only one. They are the gentle voices of reason and wisdom. Voices of enlightenment. The ones who know that, in reality, they are spiritual beings who seek to live simply and sustain life by practices that conserve the eco-systems of the world as minimally changed as humanly possible. They are drawn to the simplicity of being members of a society and community of equals – one single family of humanity across the world. And they are drawn by the inner voice of the spirit whose values are not the divisive, destructive ones of material and capital, but of harmonious participation in the Oneness of the great web of life and being throughout the universe. I hesitate to use a term commonly used by a controversial, prominent political figure, but we are in the grip of what may be called 'fake economics'.

A Zen master said this:

If there is light in the soul, there will be beauty in the person,

If there is beauty in the person, there will be harmony in the house,

If there is harmony in the house, there will be order in the nation,

If there is order in the nation, there will be peace in the world.

Inherent in the above expression, and in many similar sentiments embedded in all sensible religion and philosophy, is the Truth that will free us from the destruction we have created and in which we languish today. There must be acknowledgment of, and guidance from, the spirit and its inherent, life-giving light. We are hearing about the United States' plans for a 'Space Force'. Yet another fear-driven reaction that will not enhance peace one iota, because there is not first *light in the soul and beauty in the person*.

What follows are some considerations that may encourage us towards a new way of being – or, rather, a return to the original way designed for us. This is not complex or new. It is, simply, what we have forgotten and what we must *re-member;* what we must put back into our personal and corporate 'members' – our hearts, souls, minds and bodies – if life on planet earth is to continue and flourish.

And there is an essential sequence for this remembering. We have tried unsuccessfully to manage the affairs of life primarily using the mind and the body. We have wrongly allowed our mental faculties to assume the role of executive. And our mental faculties – as wonderful and amazing as they are – are not competent to effectively carry out that function. Why? Because, at our Centre – our truest Self – we are not mind and body. Those two are merely qualities of a deeper, more profound, more mysterious 'Self'. The words 'heart, soul, spirit' are often associated with this deeper Self. They are higher qualities than mind and body. Although it is neither possible nor wise to separate one quality from another – they all belong in a 'whole' – it can be sensibly argued that human volition or *will* – when it is directed to life-giving action – is taking its motivation from awareness arising in the heart and spirit. The function of mind and body is to be servant rather than master. We must look for direction to the deep resources of heart and spirit. The intellect is incapable of connecting us to Truth.

One wisdom tradition puts it like this: *Beyond the senses is the mind, beyond the mind is reason, beyond reason is Truth.* (Katha Upanishad)

The will directed to the search for truth is inextricably linked to the action of the spirit; that deepest, inner, mysterious *fund* of our humanness, the will being the primary faculty of the spirit.

Every 'people' – and every person within that people, whether they accept and engage with it or not – has a concept of God; a concept of spirit, the mystery behind and in and through their existence. It is impossible to speak sensibly and authoritatively about humanity and the natural order without addressing ourselves to that great, mysterious, ineffable reality. Because this entity that the peoples of the world refer to as God, by one name or another, *is* mystery, it is also impossible for anyone to claim they have the right and true understanding of God. A spiritually-wise old man I knew always began his teaching with the statement, *'I may be wrong'*. When he had finished teaching, he would again say, *'I may be wrong'*. Humility is a primary indicator of true wisdom and deep, mature humanity. It is stronger than strength, because it cannot be overcome. And, as it works to unite rather than to divide, it demonstrates its superiority over cleverness or power of one kind or another.

I remember a story told of a violent, tyrannical ruler who was terrorising his people, stealing from them, killing them, exercising absolute control over them. When people heard he was coming, they would flee for their lives and hide wherever they could. This tyrant came to one village and all the people had fled. Except for an old monk. He stood his ground humbly and resolutely before the tyrant who said to him: *'Don't you know who I am? Don't you know that I have the power to kill you'?* The old monk said to the tyrant, *'Don't you know who I am? Don't you know that I have the power to allow you to kill me'?*

Sadly, in our world today there are still such tyrants – and terrorists of one kind or another – driven by the same fear and madness. And there is still a person like the old monk inside each of us if we learn to be drawn by the power of love and life instead of fear and death. The absence of effective teaching and learning about this deepest reality is the reason for every fear, every division, every dispute, every act of aggression throughout this world.

In what follows, there is further reference to God, spirit, soul in my limited appreciation of what that signifies. There simply *has* to be. Our problems are not being solved by any of the approaches we currently use. It follows that there *is* no solution unless we embrace the possibility of something beyond our current selves; unless we submit to not knowing what to do, and surrender to the mystery of our deepest nature that we somehow know is love. Again, wisdom tells us that true knowing is only possible through loving.

I encourage you not to let the God-word deflect you from the process of opening yourself to the wonderful and terrible mystery of your life, and the impact it may have on you and on the entire world. The wisest women and men of all history – the ones who have made the most radical and life-giving contributions – have drawn their insight from that mysterious reality that we may term God or Spirit.

To live well, we need to live intentionally. We need to reflect on the worth, and be grateful for this gift of life. It's easy to say be grateful. Millions of lives are anything but pleasant. Multitudes of our sisters and brothers daily face starvation, oppression, abuse, privation of all kinds, destruction and death. And, like the old monk, each of them and each of us is able to choose – albeit many with greater difficulty than others – to abandon ourselves to that inner life that nothing can take from us, even in death.

So, how shall we live? How shall we direct our wills for the days allotted to us? For such direction determines whether we produce life or death whilst we are alive.

What follows are some thoughts on this question.

Willingly. Accept the mystery and wonder of life as a gift. Accept that life is hard, we will die, we have little control. Accept that we're really not very significant in the scheme of the universe, although we each have a great, equal, and immeasurable worth as well, and our life isn't even about us. Accept that we belong to life; we have no rights apart from being loved – a right denied so many and so often by unenlightened others. We are designed and required to love which, in turn, produces an environment in which we may also experience being loved. But we can't require others to love us. We have no control over anything except what we choose to do; what we *will*. We are not the centre of the universe. We are like an electron orbiting a nucleus; drawn to, held by and in, and an inextricable, dynamic part of the 'One', having a small but crucial role in the scheme of things. We each have the power to choose; to *will*. This quality – this ability – is our primary and greatest faculty. If we choose to exercise our will towards our true nature – to the *love* that we are at our Centre – we will be life-givers. To not 'will' to love, we remain in love's opposite; we remain in fear that creates death and destruction. Wisdom tells us that death and life are put before us each day, and we are both equipped and encouraged to choose life.

We live in very troubled and dangerous times. Our refusal to acknowledge any power greater than ourselves has meant that we rejected the very resources that make life possible and beautiful; the inner resources of heart and spirit. The result is that depression, anxiety and a host of other mental and emotional disorders are increasing alarmingly, and sufferers have nothing effective in their personal arsenal with which to combat this destructive malady. Tragically, many in the healing and health professions either seem to know nothing of this pivotal reality or – for reasons best known to themselves – fail to access it in their well-meant but often unsuccessful endeavours to heal.

Faithfully. It has been said that *the person who stands for nothing will fall for anything*. Be determined to find the only reality big enough to believe in and give you life and meaning – not money, prestige, fleeting pleasure, knowledge or power – but rather believe in the transcendent spirit reality in and though the universe. The eternal, existential truth who alone can generate life in all its fullness. There is a catch, though. To take hold of this Great Reality is not within our power. We cannot decide or choose to be 'faithful'. Rather, faith is a gift for us to seek, hear, *will to* receive and respond with a 'yes'. As we are able to do that, we are then enabled to obediently entrust our whole self freely to this mysterious God who reveals life and truth. It is to freely assent to the truth revealed by the Spirit. Our human way is to understand in order to believe. The only effective way – the way of the spirit – is to believe in order to understand. The latter way is to be and to live faithfully. Grace, commitment, submission to God, to spirit, come first. Understanding follows.

Hopefully. One great book of Wisdom – the Bible - says that only three things remain when all else passes away: faith, hope and love. These three permeate and occupy every cell of our being and knowing. They are central, inextricable aspects of our common, divine humanity. They are closest to our 'god-likeness'. Hope cannot be defeated. Hope is the source of motivation for the will. The will chooses to hope and is energised by hope. Although hope is future- focused, it enables and empowers us to be in the present, moment by moment.

Lovingly. By practising the correct relationship with our God – by being present in and committed to living from our Centre – we are enabled to develop our natural inner design, call and desire to give love regardless of it being deserved by human standards, or requested by nature. Choosing to be merciful and loving makes us truly human and gives us an experience of being at one with life. An experience of control of our personal self to the extent that is possible. The Bible tells us that we are made in the image of God, that God is Love. Love is our image. And Love encompasses faith and hope, whilst their distinct qualities and functions remain. When we are living fully, our lives will be characterised by these three: faith, hope and love.

Enthusiastically. The origin of the word is from Greek *'en Theos'* meaning 'in-God'. When we are 'in-God' – in the Truth of our very essence – we have all the resources of abundant, rich, full, life-giving life within us. We are designed and equipped to express inwardly and outwardly with integrity and energy all that is in our hearts, souls, bodies and minds. The joy, the bliss, the glory, the achievement, the celebration, the light, and including the 'shadowy side' of our natures

– the folly, the noise, the grief, the pain, the struggle, the 'dark night' of becoming. Enthusiasm is infectious, because life produces life. The more we are alive, the more we are able to receive still more life for the purpose of enjoying and giving away! The more we give away, the more we receive in the inexhaustible inner supply.

Gratefully. Being thankful to the Source of Life for everything. See every moment, every event, every aspect of life, as an opportunity for individual and communal gratefulness in ways that are honouring to the spirit within the self, within others, and within the universe. Being grateful is a life-giving choice. Faced with what we have been given and cannot change, our options are to accept gratefully and experience peace and contentment, or to resist and experience resentment and turmoil.

Humbly. Make every effort to know who we really are and, as much as it is possible to know, who God really is, so that we see correctly and assume the correct attitude to relationship with God, Self, others, this world of creatures, and matter of the universe. Relate to all with awe and honour. Humility is a powerful, prominent indicator of true presence; of a soul in unity with self, others and the universe. *'When I see a good man, I strive to be like him; when I see an evil man, I consider my own condition'. (Confucius)*

Truthfully. What does it mean to live truthfully if not to be fully who we are. To be manifesting every aspect of our amazing being, interacting with all other creatures in our known universe in the attitude of awe, and honour for all life and creation. When Jesus said, *'I am the way and the 'truth' and the life' (John 16:6)*, what did he mean if not to be as he was and is beyond all constraints of time as we know it?

One with the One Spirit whom he called 'daddy', a loving, honouring, accepting, authentic childlike 'being with' all that is without attachment or agenda other than to 'be' and to 'love'. Living truthfully in this way annihilates deceit, falsehood, separation of one from another.

Courageously. Don't settle for politeness – political correctness – when truth is required to bring life and freedom. Honourably, humbly, supportively challenge everything that is less than the glory of Truth intended by God for our highest good and for the same in all others. When we live in Truth, there is nothing to fear. There is nothing that can take anything from us that is worth anything. Courage is the result.

Mindfully. Develop practices that direct us to live deliberately and with awareness in each present, eternal moment. Be aware of breathing each breath, hearing each sound, seeing each hue, smelling each scent, feeling each sensation. Meditate, contemplate, pray, reflect, be alertly and fully present to what is. Surrender the body, mind, emotions to the deep, mysterious, inner reality of spirit. Attach to nothing of the physical world. Hold everything reverently and lightly, engaging with and enjoying deeply all that is good and, at the same time, letting it go. For nothing here can be truly held. In this way, be in control of yourself, rather than being controlled by other people, circumstances or events.

Simply. Use what is physically necessary to sustain a healthy body, mind and spirit. Contain the temptation and pressure to busyness of thought, speech, action and acquisition. Beyond a certain level of what is necessary to live with dignity and to experience the richness of a gentle life, less is generally more. To live simply, is to make it possible for others to also live with human dignity and sufficiency.

Economically. Develop awareness of treading lightly on the earth. Use its resources carefully and sparingly. Consume only what is necessary to sustain your being and that of all others on the earth. We Australians use 7.5 hectares per capita of resources. The global average is 2.5. Be also economic with your words, gestures, actions, thoughts, desires, wants. Listen much. Speak little.

Generously. Be uneconomic only in your giving. Give surplus away joyfully. Give joyfully when there is no surplus. Look for opportunities to be extravagant with giving of all that we are and have, and experience the pleasure to be found in that. We can properly possess nothing in this life. We die and whatever we possessed remains for someone else. So give and, in doing so, the miracle of receiving is initiated. It is written that *'It is more blessed to give than to receive' (Acts 20:35).* Giving activates an inner knowing that all is well with the soul and all that one is. Kahlil Gibran said, *'Let the season of your giving be yours and not your inheritor's'. (The Prophet).* Everything we have been given is for the purpose of sharing it with others.

Peacefully. Francis of Assisi lived a life of simple, profound unity with himself and all that is. The Prayer of St Francis reflects this: *Lord, make me an instrument of your peace. Where there is hatred, let me sow love, where there is injury, pardon, where there is doubt, faith, where there is despair, hope, where there is darkness, light, where there is sadness, joy. Divine Master, grant that I may not so much seek to be consoled as to console, to be understood as to understand, to be loved as to love. For it is in giving that we receive, it is in pardoning that we are pardoned, and* *it is in dying that we are born to eternal life*. Peace is our central nature; our natural state. Peace is a humble acceptance and gentle resting. In the words of another well-known prayer by Reinhold Niebuhr, it is *'The serenity to accept what we cannot change, the courage to change what we can, and the wisdom to know the difference'*. Being at peace is being content; being 'at one' with our content, with all that is our life.

Restoratively. Serving and giving to the total environment rather than only being served and taking from it. Planting trees, recycling matter, disposing of minimised waste thoughtfully and sustainably, modelling, teaching and encouraging others by example and exhortation. Develop skills of resourcefulness. Experience the pleasure in repairing, re-engineering, re-using materials and implements that have been broken and discarded.

Graciously. Acknowledging that we all do wrong and none of us can justify judging or condemning another. Whatever darkness exists in another, our unwavering value and acceptance of the worth of that other will be the light that removes the darkness from them and, in the process, from ourselves. Grace is a gift of acceptance that we cannot, and are not required to, earn. It is a gentle, honouring, secure 'resting in our acceptability'. Grace is received abundantly and freely and is to be given in the same extravagant way.

Forgivingly. For you to forgive is not for the benefit of the one who has done wrong. For you to forgive is for *you!* It is to release *you* from the pain of the wrong and cause you to experience freedom again. Your freedom also facilitates the release of the other from the damage caused to them by their wrong behaviour. Your forgiveness demonstrates to them the life-giving power within each of us to release ourselves and each other from all burdens. A dear friend of mine was estranged from his father for twenty years. They lived on opposites sides of the world. My friend finally realised his need to forgive his father so he could be free of the pain he carried. In deep, humble conviction, he did so. The *next day* his father phoned him saying *'Matthew (not his real name), is everything alright; I felt a strange urge to contact you'*? Whatever you bind on earth is bound in heaven; whatever you loose on earth is loosed in heaven (Matthew 16:19).

Responsibly. We are One and part of the One. When a brother, sister, or creature suffers, I suffer – even though I may not feel it. We are their care-giver/keeper; their servants. In adulthood, we are each totally responsible for ourselves and jointly responsible for each other and all of the natural order. 'I am responsible' are three of the most important, releasing, empowering and life-giving words we can utter. These words put me in control of my life, but not independently of others. Responsibility puts the good of the community ahead of my own good.

Justly. Know the difference between lawful processes and justice. It can be vast. Realise that justice is not complete justice if it fails to restore individuals to themselves, others, and their communities. Know that restoration begins for perpetrator and victim alike when the perpetrator demonstrates awareness of, and remorse for, the harm they have caused. When they express complete responsibility for their personal actions, unflinchingly take whatever action is within their power to make restitution and, where possible, be reconciled to those they have hurt and to the wider community. Speak and act justly in all matters and, where social justice – be it local, national, or international

– is being compromised, speak for those who don't have a voice, act for those who don't have power. Make your goal to reconcile, heal, restore all to fullness of life.

Sustainably. Actively seek to develop and employ in our homes and workplaces technologies and practices that are not harmful to life and creation. Actions that are not based on depleting the finite resources of the planet, nor unsustainably adding unnatural waste to the eco-systems of this fragile and beautiful earth home. In nature, there is no waste. In nature, there is perfect balance. We need to learn from, and emulate, that phenomenon in order for there to be a livable future. We need to repair, restore, re-plant, free rivers to flow, stop producing compounds that won't interact harmoniously with the natural environment.

Communally. Actively seek to be part of each other's lives whilst honouring the unique personhood and privacy of self and each other. Sharing your presence, relationship, energies, doubts, opinions, hopes, dreams, fears, joy, meals, tasks, equipment, burdens. Being together enables us to grow into who we were designed to become. The 'rough edges' of our raw material get rubbed off each of us. We learn to accept, accommodate, adjust, adapt, deepen, become patient, kind, durable, resilient, rich in personhood, rich in divine, mature humanity.

Patiently. The Bible tells us (Galatians 5:22-23) that *'the fruit of the Spirit is love, joy, peace, patience, kindness, goodness, faithfulness, gentleness, self- control'*. Where these qualities are, there is the Spirit in the person. There is the deepest Self. Where these qualities are not present, there is a lack in that being. Who amongst us would choose *not* to experience these qualities in our life? Why would we choose to be ruled by the blind and self-deluding ego and deny ourselves the richest of life's pleasures?

Joyfully. Joy is another choice made possible by choosing to live by the spirit. Every day, life and death – joy and sorrow – are put before us. We are encouraged to choose life and, with that choice, sorrow is enabled to dissolve into joy. Of course, as we are human, we each automatically experience sorrow at losses we suffer through life. That is normal for us. But when we allow sorrow to remain, we are choosing to prolong unnecessary suffering. Sorrow well! Grieve well! Then, at the time that is right for us, choose to return to joy, our natural, spiritual state.

Visionarily. Deliberately set our heart, soul, mind and strength on the great, mysterious vision of the eternal, transcendent spirit mystery we may call God who is all, in all, before all, beyond all and who calls from within and empowers us to be actively one with that indivisible One. From that One Vision, all other valid visions will emerge. *We have no rest until we find our rest in God (Augustine of Hippo)*

Silently. Make adequate spaces for silence and stillness outwardly, in order to develop the great, life-giving silence and stillness inwardly in all of life's circumstances. Seek a life-giving measure of solitude to give greater value to your engagement with community. Remember the words of the wise Jean Vanier: *'If you fear solitude, beware of community; if you fear community, beware of solitude'*. We each have the capacity and need to become equally content in either state.

Uncommon sense

- We each have the power to choose; to 'will'. This quality is our primary and greatest faculty. If we choose to exercise our will towards love – our true nature – we will be 'life-givers'; if we fail to choose love, we will be 'life-takers'.

- Faith is a gift for us to seek truth, hear, receive and respond with a 'yes'. The way of the ego is to understand in order to believe; the way of the spirit is to believe in order to understand.

- Wisdom says that only three things remain when all else passes away: faith, hope and love. Although hope is future-focused, it enables and empowers us to be securely present, moment by moment.

- Love is our True Image. By being present in and committed to living from our Centre – our spirit – we are enabled to develop our natural inner design, call and desire to give love regardless of it being deserved by human standards, or requested by nature.

- When we are in God (*en Theos*) – in our truest Self – we have all the resources of abundant, rich, full, life-giving life within us. Enthusiasm is infectious because life produces life.

- Be thankful to the Creator Spirit for everything. If 'what is' can't be changed, our options are to accept gratefully and experience peace and contentment, or resist and experience resentment and turmoil.

- Humility is being neither beneath nor above our True Selves.

- What does it mean to live truthfully if not to be fully who we are. Living truthfully annihilates deceit, falsehood, separation of one from another.
- When we live in truth, there is nothing to fear. There is nothing that can take anything of value from us. Courage is the result.
- Develop practices that direct us to live deliberately and with awareness in each present, eternal moment. Meditate, contemplate, pray, reflect, be alertly and fully present to what is.
- To live simply is to make it possible for others to also live with human dignity and sufficiency.
- Use the earth's resources carefully and sparingly.
- Give surplus away joyfully. Give joyfully when there is no surplus. Everything we have been given is for the purpose of sharing it with others.
- Peace is our central nature; our natural state. Peace is the humble acceptance and gentle resting.
- Experience pleasure in repairing, re-engineering materials, implements and people that have been broken and discarded.
- Grace is a gift of acceptance that we cannot – and are not required – to earn.
- To forgive is to release you from the pain of the wrong and cause you to experience freedom again. It also facilitates the release of the one who has wronged you.
- In adulthood, we are totally responsible for ourselves and jointly responsible for each other and all of the natural order.

- Justice is not complete justice if it fails to restore individuals to themselves, others and their communities.
- Develop and employ technologies and practices that are not harmful to life and the earth.
- Seek to be part of each other's lives whilst honouring the unique personhood and privacy of each other and of self.
- Patience is one sign of a person living in their spirit.
- Joy is another choice made possible by choosing to live from the spirit Centre.
- Deliberately set our heart, soul, mind and strength on the great, mysterious, transcendent reality that we may call God.
- Make adequate spaces for silence and stillness outwardly, in order to develop life-giving silence and stillness inwardly in all of life's circumstances.

Self-responsibility and blaming

Choosing to live in the ways mentioned above calls us to be responsible for ourselves rather than to find fault and apportion blame.

As we've said before, the ego finds it extremely unpleasant to be thought to be 'wrong', and will defend itself – often vehemently – if challenged. As mentioned before, the ego has developed an arsenal of defences against being wrong, and employs them rigorously to keep itself feeling 'right' whether it's right or not. The ego seems hell-bent – literally – on finding someone to blame when anything occurs that is uncomfortable for it. When caught out reacting to some event, the ego will try to justify, rationalise, project, displace, etc., so it feels it is not to blame. Johnnie's ego says, *'It's his fault; if he hadn't said 'x', I wouldn't have done 'y''!* Doing 'y' is the responsibility of Johnnie. No-one caused him to do it. No-one but him is responsible for it.

How often do we experience similar situations, and how painful it is to say *'I'm sorry. I shouldn't have done that. I was wrong. Please forgive me'*. It is only the spirit – the Centre – who is able, readily and willingly, to accept complete personal responsibility for its part in any conflict. It's important to be clear we are not advocating taking full responsibility for the *whole* event, only for *our part* in the event.

In any difference of opinion or argument, there are two participants. Obviously, each plays a part, and some aspects of those 'parts' are likely to be reproachable. No-one is perfect! So, to resolve any hurt caused during an unpleasant or hurtful interchange, it is always good to say,

'I apologise for my part' and mean it. The ego isn't capable of doing that. Only the spirit is able to. That's where we need to increasingly live.

My experience as psychotherapist over decades has made me acutely aware of the troublesome ego and the redeeming spirit. In therapy – or any relationship, really – it is quite usual for a contract to begin with blame: *'My husband is impossible to live with; he's the problem in our marriage'!* *'My wife doesn't understand me'*. In contrast, towards the end of a therapy contract some years ago, I remember one of my clients – a young mother – saying, *'My kid's been a bit ratty lately; I need to take a look at myself'*. This wise young mother had begun living from her newly-conscious, self-responsible spirit!

Uncommon sense

- Accept the truth that even though you are not perfect you are an acceptable human being worth as much as any other human being.
- Your ego will resist accepting that it is ever wrong.
- You will make mistakes. It is normal. It's ok. Making mistakes doesn't diminish your worth in any way.
- It is truly human and mature to acknowledge, admit, accept personal responsibility for errors of judgment and behaviours, apologise and bring relationship with yourself and the other back into livable harmony.
- *'I am responsible'* are three of the most helpful, healing and adult words you can say.

Interior maintenance: finding wisdom

Our personal responsibility for our lives requires that *we* do the required maintenance on ourselves; that *we* seek the wisdom we need to run our lives appropriately.

In our modern Western lives of constant mobility, rapid succession of images, plethora of activities, new information, fads and pressure to keep up with the latest whatever, wisdom doesn't get much of a look in. There is no shortage of information and knowledge, presented as real, important and necessary. But information and knowledge are as distinct from wisdom as chalk is from cheese. We say a whole lot more than we believe. And we believe a whole lot more than we do. And we know a whole lot more than we could ever put into practice. Unless our lives are congruent with our stated philosophies, our words are worthless and our lives are fake. Information and knowledge have their uses. But bringing us to life-giving wisdom is not one of them. We need to question rather than thoughtlessly abdicate personal responsibility, and follow the herd over the edge into the abyss. As mentioned earlier, the state of the world attests to that reality. What we're doing is working against life not for it. Where, then, can we find wisdom?

The ancients, and the modern wise women and men of varying philosophies and religions, show us that wisdom is to be found beyond the senses, beyond the mind and even beyond reason. They show more than they tell because, to be wisdom, it has to be embodied. It has to be lived experience. It's one thing to say prayers, for example. It is another thing entirely to be *prayerful*. It is one thing to hold a view contrary to your community. It is another thing altogether to live out that view.

Wisdom has been around as long as human beings have been aware of what we might call *enlightenment*; that ability to discern that we are more than merely feeling, thinking, acting beings. We are spiritual beings who have an inner life that is more profound, more mysterious, yet more real than anything else we are. And there are many paths and ways of seeking that wisdom that comes from within. Some have been with us for several thousand years and are as valid today as they were when first discovered or created.

One increasingly popular path is that of Buddhism. Buddha Siddhartha Gautama founded Buddhism around 540 B.C. He taught disciples to seek enlightenment via practice of the Noble Eightfold Path: right thought, right speech, right action, right livelihood, right effort, right mindfulness, right concentration (or meditation), right understanding. But, in part, Buddhism's popularity is that it doesn't teach or require submission to any higher power. For those seeking an encounter with the mysterious source of life and desiring to experience a *personal* connectedness to one they may like to think of as God, the Buddhist path – with all that is of great value to life – is unlikely to satisfy.

One of several God-centred approaches worthy of mention here is that of the *Rule of Benedict*. Discerned and formalised by a layman, Benedict – now known as Saint Benedict – between 500 and 540 A.D., *The Rule*, as it is known, became the norm for monastic living throughout Europe and the world, and remains so to this day. The Rule promotes balance in the way seekers design their lives.

For Benedict, the essential activities were regular study of scripture, prayer, reflection (holy leisure), work, and service within community. If compared to the Eight-Fold Path, for example, the Rule contains the same elements but with the notable – and I believe essential – addition of submission of the ego-self to the deeper, inner reality of the spirit; the *spirit-essence* powering and informing our substance. The mysterious yet real source of life and all that is. That reality that we may call God within us. The key requirement for us to experience being secure and significant is the paradox of surrender to that inner spirit. The deepest spiritual paths agree that we must abandon our need for control in order to achieve control. Of course, our ego rails at this as a preposterous suggestion and resists vehemently. Wisdom tells us that any path that doesn't lead to such surrender leaves us short of being fully human. Leaves us short of being able to relate appropriately to ourselves, each other and our earth. In this surrender, I engage with my own spirit and reap all the benefits of the divine/human mystery.

To find wisdom, we must necessarily seek out wisdom literature. For Benedict, that meant the Holy Scriptures; the Bible. The heart and spirit are directed in humble surrender to God as the mind engages the divine revelation in Scripture. Scripture is reflected upon, is the focus for contemplation and the foundation for prayer. The purpose of prayer is not to get God to do what I ask for. Rather, it is to transform the one praying into the fullness of their being; into their God-image. Study, contemplation and prayer are interspersed by physical labour and service to one's community members. All members of the monastic community are equal in status and all serve one another. There is no partiality. Although, if and when needed, the Abbot has the responsibility of being the final arbiter after full discussion with, and consideration of, all community members.

Although not the only worthy model, this Rule fulfils the requirements for successful, meaningful life. It is not only for monastic communities. Each one of us – even the busiest mothers, office or industry workers – can find adequate time for the activities in the Rule. We don't have to stop work to think, reflect, pray or serve. We don't need to be in church or our meditation space. God is not confined to time or space. Our places and times of daily occupation can embody all essential activities to lead us into Godly, human maturity.

The only thing we must have is the realisation of our need for God in order to fulfil our design. To become who we really are. And, of course, that realisation is useless without our commitment to give ourselves fully to it. The important thing for us to remember when we're talking about surrender or submission is that it doesn't mean we're giving up, giving in, giving way, or losing anything we may think of as worth in ourselves. The absolute reverse is the case that will be experienced! This God to whom we submit is not in the business of spoiling pleasure or controlling us. Rather, God within is in the business of providing joy and freedom beyond our wildest imaginations here in this life, as well as whatever life there is to come.

Uncommon sense

- Information and knowledge have their uses. But bringing us to life-giving wisdom is not one of them.

- Wise women and men of varying philosophies and religions show us that wisdom is to be found beyond the senses, beyond the mind and even beyond reason. They *show* more than they *tell* because, to be wisdom, it has to be embodied. It has to be lived experience.

- Wisdom discerns that we are more than mere thinking, feeling, acting beings. We are spiritual beings who have an inner life that is more profound, more mysterious, yet more real than anything else we are.

- Wisdom requires the submission of the ego to the deeper, inner reality of the *spirit essence* powering and informing our substance.

- We must abandon our need to control in order to achieve control.

- Wisdom tells us that any path that doesn't lead to such surrender leaves us short of being fully human. Surrender doesn't mean giving in, giving up, giving way or losing anything we may think of as *worth* in ourselves.

- To find wisdom we need to seek out and study wisdom literature, contemplate, pray, meditate, engage in communities of equality and impartiality, labour together for the common good.

- We don't have to stop work to think, pray, reflect or serve. We don't need to be in our church, mosque, temple, synagogue or meditation place.

- The only thing we must have is the realisation of our need for God in order to fulfil our design.

Part Three:

Society's organisation and beyond

Corporatism and the displacement of the citizen

The resources of the world are finite. The economics of corporatism demands infinite growth which, in this finite system is, simply, impossible, irrational and, in the words of Schumacher and so many others, insane! Yet we continue to 'stampede' forward, naively believing that 'science and technology will find a solution' to the myriad problems we are creating by our blindness and irresponsibility. The unbelievably mindless belief that coal can be made 'clean' is just one example of our folly. No matter how finely you grind coal, no matter how many impurities you remove from it, when it combines with oxygen and burns, it still produces a mass of atmosphere-warming carbon dioxide. It cannot be made clean. Yet we believe the lies we are fed by the ones who own and control the coal business, and the politicians who do their bidding. There are myriad examples of deceit – either by well-intentioned ignorance, or by deliberate, evil manipulation for personal gain at the expense of others and of the earth. We will consider some of these later.

Is there a solution to our present and rapidly deteriorating interaction with our material home, planet earth, and all its people – our brothers and sisters, both human and other? Throughout history, there have been innumerable diligent attempts to solve the problems of our creating. Their failure to have any significant effect is due to the fact that, as Einstein stated, *'a problem cannot be solved with the same consciousness that created it'*. We are trying to prevent poverty through wealth acquisition; we are trying to bring peace through violence; we are trying to bring unity through hierarchy and division, equality through discrimination, fairness through privilege, love through fear, freedom through oppression. We will not succeed until we abandon our present mode of being – and the consciousness that spawned it – and replace it with one that is congruent with goals that serve the common good.

Corporatism is a 'lie become truth'. Arguably, corporatism was born in the late seventeen hundreds with the industrial revolution. When mechanisation usurped the roles previously carried out by men and women, a dramatic shift occurred. Certainly some of the drudgery was taken over by machines. But, more significantly, the ordinary citizen workers lost their legitimacy as *the* unit of production for society. Machines, and the corporate system they accompanied, became the locus of legitimacy. When workers were the primary contributors to the operation of their societies, they had power. With the arrival of technology, that power shifted from worker-citizens to the elite and their capital. That shift remains and has become entrenched to the point that it is not even challenged anymore; it is not even recognised as a debilitating reality.

We know that democracy is government of the people by the people or their representatives for the benefit of the people, i.e. *'the greatest good for the greatest number'* of citizens. Corporatism is a system in which private individuals and groups own the means of production and distribution and associated information and language for the express purpose of acquiring personal profit. Wealth, with its power and influence, is concentrated in the hands of a few. To be fair to those who own the corporate system, they may well believe this arrangement is the only option for the ordering of our societies. They have accepted the deception of themselves and all of us that the 'free markets' must not be interfered with. The markets must be allowed to have their head and be self-regulating.

The fact is, corporatism is the result of human unconsciousness, the associated lack of awareness of what is happening in and around us, and of the destructive effects and injustice it perpetrates on this world. Those who benefit from corporatism – called the 1%-ers, shall we say – and the 99%-ers have all unconsciously accepted that 'this is how it is and must be'. This unfair, unsustainable, inhuman system is not challenged by anyone, and so it continues unabated. The reason? We have stopped thinking! In fact, generally, we haven't started thinking! We haven't been taught or encouraged to think, because thinking would almost certainly challenge the status quo and upset the smooth-running of the injustice. We have been educated, trained, brainwashed – or, more appropriately, 'brain-sullied' – by the corporatist view characterising every institution.

Our education system (in Australia, at least) teaches a variety of useful and essential skills, and a great deal of information, but it fails to teach about common humanity and how to 'think'. The standardised NAPLAN system teaches and prepares all student nationwide for pre-set tests. When we get good results, we think we have a successful education system. Not so! All we have done is to produce a bunch of kids who can learn stuff and pass tests! TAFE (Technical And Further Education) does pretty well in providing practical training for employment, and that is essential and should be funded more generously than it is.

But universities are also training students for occupations, many of which will be obsolete before the students graduate. Corporatism has so infiltrated universities that students are not being taught to 'think'. Students are being prepared to take their places in the management of the corporatist delusion. We'll talk more about this later.

Sitting uncomfortably with corporatism is what we are led to believe is democracy. It is an impossible marriage. These diametrically opposed systems clearly indicate that we can have either corporatism or democracy, but we can't have both. They are mutually exclusive! Yet we are burdened by successive waves of politicians who mindlessly accept the lie that *'the market forces ruling the corporatist system must not be interfered with'* and, further, that *'we live in a 'robust democracy'!* To further insult our intelligence, the perhaps well-meaning but ignorant purveyors of corporatism seem to believe and act as if it is possible to have *infinite growth in a finite, closed system of resources called planet earth!* I find it perplexing and tragic that they can't see the stupidity in holding to such a stance. I feel deep concern for future generations who will inherit from us a perhaps irredeemable social and geological environment in which to exist.

In these present times, it seems that ordinary citizens the world over are becoming increasingly disempowered, increasingly disenchanted with politicians and political structures that are clearly not serving humanity or the earth generally. Not only is the corporatist mentality destroying the natural world on which we all rely totally for our very existence, it is causing accelerating and widespread suffering as the very social fabric of humanity disintegrates; as our erstwhile-valued humanity has been replaced by economics.

Uncommon sense

- Continuous growth in a finite system is impossible, irrational, insane.

- As a society, we continue to stampede onwards without concern for the destruction of eco-systems, mindlessly believing that 'science will find a solution' to the problems we are creating.

- One example is the illusion that coal can be made 'clean' *(although CO_2 can be captured at the 'stack', the energy required renders the idea untenable)*.

- We fail to solve our problems because, as Einstein stated, *'a problem cannot be solved with the same consciousness that created it'*.

- Personal wealth acquisition won't solve poverty; violence won't create peace; hierarchy and division won't create unity; discrimination won't create equality; privilege won't create fairness; fear won't create love; oppression won't create freedom.

- Corporatism is a lie that has become truth.

- Born in the industrial revolution, mechanisation usurped the roles of women and men. Ordinary citizen workers lost their legitimacy as *the essential* units of production and primary contributors to their societies; they lost their power to the elite and their capital.

- Corporatism is now entrenched and little-challenged as 'priority citizen'.

- Corporatism and democracy are mutually exclusive. Democracy asks the greatest good for the greatest number; corporatism demands unfettered acquisition of wealth for the few who own the means of production and consumption.

- Those who own, sustain and benefit from the so-called 'free-market' system falsely claim that it must not be interfered with; it must be allowed to have its head and self-regulate. Part of the lie.

- Corporatism is the destructive result of human unconsciousness. The purveyors of corporatism are either unaware or flagrantly dismissive of the destruction being visited upon the earth and all its inhabitants.

- Our education system fails to teach about common humanity; how to *be* and how to think about existence.

- Corporatism has so infiltrated universities that students are not adequately taught how to think critically; and many are simply prepared to take their place in the corporate delusion.

Economics

In its most basic definition, economics is about the production and distribution of goods and services needed to sustain human life. In its purest form, economics is an essential 'good'– a benefit – for all concerned. Those who produce specific goods or services are enabled to trade them for goods and services they cannot provide themselves, thereby facilitating all goods and services to be available to all individuals as each has need. As societies grew in size and complexity, and scattered themselves over ever wider areas, trading became more difficult to effect. Money was created to be a medium of exchange, and goods and services were increasingly 'traded' for money which was then traded for all needed goods and services.

As long as humans have walked the earth, we have been beset by this inherent 'flaw' – this essential and useful yet diabolical 'ego' which affects every aspect of our lives. Economics is not immune! As we have emphasised throughout this book, the ego is flawed by unconsciousness and, thus, fear. And fear distorts the good implementation of economics. Fear is concerned with lack – lack of control, lack of essentials to sustain life, lack of a sense of personal value and security, etc. The result in the lives of those who, for various reasons (skill, opportunity, location, aptitude, attitude, etc.), have access to goods and services, is accumulation of goods beyond what is needed, and overuse of services thus denying access to those services for many others.

Greed and consumption become rampant – and the norm – and the gap between the 'haves' and the 'have-nots' continues to widen. These days we are hearing about the '1%' of 'haves' versus the '99%' of 'have nots'. In reality, those percentages are indicative only. In actuality, the wealth is more likely to be in the hands of far fewer than 1% of the world's population, and the struggle is the reality of far more than 99%. When six of the richest men in the United States have a combined personal wealth equivalent to that of 3.5 billion of the world's poorest – just under half of the population of the world – what does that say about the morality of corporatism? To 'make America great again', as mindlessly ranted by a US President, that inequity and the soulless attitudes and policies that created it will need to be dramatically redressed.

The economic system that the wealthy and powerful have developed for their own self-interest, and that the majority of us have allowed to develop to our great detriment, is fatally flawed. As control of the production and distribution of goods and services has devolved into the hands of fewer individuals and corporations, the system that was designed to be our servant has become our master. And a tyrannical master at that.

How can such an inequitable system – a system we know as corporatism – exist and be sustained in a nation that calls itself democratic? The fact is, it can't! As the wise young Prime Minister of New Zealand, Jacinda Ardern, has stated, *'the problem with democracy is capitalism'*. She is the only politician I have ever heard who has the wisdom to understand, and the courage to state the truth in this matter. I venture to suggest that she may have clarified further by differentiating between *capitalism* and *corporatism*.

John G. White

Capitalism – the use of capital – is essential for growth and development to provide infrastructure for our growing population. And capitalism is benign until it is captured by a philosophy (I use that term loosely here) and associated action of what is most appropriately termed *corporatism*. This is the arrangement and use of capital to create and maintain a system of wealth, power and influence that is inaccessible to the majority of the citizens of the world. Our consideration and correct understanding of the dangers of corporatism must be central to our effort if we are to redress all the major difficulties besetting the majority of human beings on this planet. Corporatism and its inextricable and unhealthy relationship with financial systems, has caused a diabolical shift of focus from people to money; from social considerations to economic ones.

It is interesting to note that for all but a few hundred years of the last 2000-odd since the birth of democracy in Greece, 'the economy' was not the topic of government concern. The primary concern and focus of democracy was good social order. 'The economy' is all that current politicians talk about. The economy has become the evil master rather than the good servant, its original design.

Is there a solution?

For several thousand years, the wise women and men – gurus, mystics, spiritual seekers of all persuasions – have been saying that we must 'return'; return to the Centre, to the Centre of our being; to the spirit – that inexpressible-but-true-reality' that indwells each individual and enables us to live as 'One' people in honour, equity and harmony. What is required for uncommon sense to return, to become common again, and for life on earth to be sustained, is transformation of the human heart. Renewing of the mind. Submission of the ego to the higher power of spirit/God. Of course, the ego vehemently resists the idea of submission, because it wrongly thinks in doing so it will lose control and become insecure. Little does it realise that *only by* surrendering is one able to enter a state of complete security and, paradoxically, absolute control – absolute freedom – of not needing to be in control!

Let me say one more thing about the folly of corporatism. As we are spiritual beings at our true Centre, and temporarily existing in this physical realm, we can't properly 'own' anything. The desire for and attempt at 'ownership' is one more folly of the ego. Rather than *owning* a thing, we are generally actually *owned by* the thing. We expend effort and money to acquire it, insure it, repair it, maintain it, worry about it being damaged or stolen. Obviously, we need certain physical resources to sustain life while we are here, and there is nothing foolish about that. But, to focus on acquisition and ownership takes us away – fatally separates us – from our true nature and, thus, prevents us from experiencing peaceful contentment and harmonious interaction with ourselves, each other and our planet home. A corollary to the dangers of acquisition is that the more we have of earth's finite resources, the less are available to some others of our brothers and sisters. To experience freedom, we need to hold everything loosely. We need to use and enjoy everything, and hold them loosely so that if and when they are broken, lost, stolen, worn out, etc., we don't suffer unnecessary pain; we don't lose contact with our souls.

Uncommon sense

- Economics – the production and distribution of goods and services – is a system created to serve our needs

- Distorted by ego, production and distribution has been concentrated in the hands of fewer individuals, and serves to physically enrich and empower the few and impoverish and disempower the many.

- Acquisition and greed result from fear of lack: lack of control of one's life, lack of security, lack of an experience of personal value as a human being.

- Because of inequitable wealth distribution of corporatism, democracy and corporatism cannot coexist; they are mutually exclusive.

- Corporatism is fatally flawed as it depends on infinite growth in a finite, physical environment; insanity! It also presupposes that the few are of greater worth than the many. This unsupportable belief divides, alienates, embitters the many, emboldens the few, and is destructive of all.

- Any workable solution must be based on our *return* to our true spiritual Centre – to consciousness – which alone is able to direct life successfully.

- Because we are spiritual beings temporarily in a physical realm, we cannot properly 'own' anything. Attempts or desires to own fatally separate us from our truest Selves, from each other, and from our planet home.

Politics or Government?

Most if not all politics and political systems are dysfunctional to some extent because, by and large, they are created and managed by the unconsciousness of the human ego. This ego has succumbed to the lie of corporatism and is, therefore, elitist and unjust.

How can I make such an outlandish statement? If politics and political systems were created by the consciousness of spirit of the human Centre (which is Love), we would be experiencing worldwide 'Oneness', equitable sharing of resources, harmony and mutually-honouring cooperation, minimal exploitation of precious, finite resources, and actual democracy. People would be valued and material used, rather than the reverse. Manipulation, oppression and abuses of all kinds would be rare. Those to whom much was given would have no excess, and those to whom little was given would have no lack. Instead, we have the elitist, inequitable, secretive, adversarial behaviour of corporatism.

Politicians would be recompensed equivalently to every other worker. They would speak truth instead of lies. They would answer yes/no questions. They would have nothing to hide. They would see themselves as servants of the people rather than as masters. Elections and the election cycles would be dramatically different. The main focus would be on the distant future rather than the next election cycle. The illusion of power would not exist. There would be no wasteful, destructive adversarialism between any parties, be they groups or individuals.

The focus would be on national and international interests rather than on any sense of 'winning power' or being superior. The primary focus – the highest good - would be human rights – restorative justice, mercy and compassion. Personal and corporate contributions to government finances would be in proportion to individual and corporate incomes. All natural resources would remain the property of the nation's citizenry, and any corporation exploiting those resources would purchase the resources at a value appropriate to the quality and quantity of the resource.

Soulful, talent-using, meaningful *livelihoods* would replace utilitarian *jobs*, good only for providing money to buy and consume. Every adult or family unit would receive an adequate living wage. Hours of work would be reduced. Homelessness would be unheard of. Dysfunctional and antisocial behaviours would be managed by the community in which they occurred. Prisons would be emptied as inmates were actually 'corrected' by being assisted to recognise and engage with their true nature and live the lives for which they were designed. Schools would first educate students in who they are as spirit-centred human beings of equal and significant worth. Bullying would be non-existent because individuals would see the one in front of them as their own self and value accordingly. Students would primarily be taught and encouraged to think and question.

Sound like utopia?

Well, maybe. And, yes, it is painting an idealistic picture. But something approaching it could result from something we might call *'communitarianism'* – not God-less socialism, communism, corporatism, or fascism, but soulful, spirit-full uniqueness of mutually-honouring individuals within community. It doesn't have to be *either/or*. It must be *both/and*. For life to work and be experienced as wonderful, the individual's uniqueness must have an honoured and equal place. But that place must also be subservient to the greater good of the community to which the individual belongs, and to which they contribute that uniqueness. Democracy demands that legitimacy resides unquestioned with the citizenry. I'll say that again: Democracy demands that legitimacy resides unquestioned with the citizenry! The greatest good for the greatest number. Capital must serve the citizen.

Why are we so far from the picture painted above?

The legitimacy I spoke about above has been usurped by corporatism! And we, the citizens of this nation, *the government of which legitimately belongs to us*, have allowed this travesty to be implemented and remain unchallenged.

The present systems of *government* (I use that term generously) largely fail in their responsibility to engage all citizens in meaningful, life-giving ways that build us, both individual and community. Why? Well, here in Australia and other western nations, politicians have confused corporatism with democracy. As mentioned elsewhere, these two systems are mutually exclusive.

We don't have democracy in Australia! We have corporatism! And, unless we wake up pretty quickly, we'll have full-blown fascism. Look at the white-supremacist leanings and connections already in a couple of major parties. Look at the inter-national connections of racism and arbitrary division. Look at the rapidly-increasing legislative controls on the masses and freedoms for the owners of capital.

Politicians talk about 'this robust democracy' whilst cutting services, wages and conditions of the marginalised, aged and poorest citizens, giving tax breaks to the rich, and allowing transnational corporations to exploit the nation's natural resources without paying appropriately for those resources and without paying tax!

It is perhaps worth noting here that the Labor government of John Curtin with Treasurer, Ben Chifley, designed and implemented the highly regulated financial system that allowed Australia to thrive industrially during the early 1940s. However, in the late 1950s, the Menzies' Liberal government orchestrated the deregulation of banking and financial services such that savings and commercial banking functions – those services required to be secure for the citizens – were no longer separated from risky investment functions of the banks. That deregulation also removed the power of the Commonwealth Bank – the people's bank – to limit interest charges of other banks, and to ensure that inter-banking and insurance arrangements did not risk the assets of the banks and, therefore, of the citizens to whom the assets belonged. Since that time, regulation of the financial systems has been by the financial systems themselves.

It is interesting that a conservative-led Banking Royal Commission of 1936 affirmed that the Federal Parliament is ultimately responsible for monetary policy and the government of the day is the executive of the Parliament. As we have seen, that ideal – a just and appropriate approach to actual governing – has long since gone. Governments since that time have handed control of monetary policy to the privately owned and operated financial sector. Curtin and Chifley also noted that if a government deliberately (or by default) excludes itself from participation in the making or changing of monetary policy, it cannot govern. That is the situation now. The Australian government is not and cannot govern. They make plenty of positive-sounding noises, but the reality is, our financial system is completely out of their (and our) control.

It's not obvious how supposedly intelligent women and men of parliament maintain that they preside over a democracy. In fact it is democracy *in name only*. What *is* obvious, though, is that their hands are tied, and they have neither the vision nor the courage to untie them.

Politicians say they are public servants. Which is true. But many act like public masters. They seem to believe it is appropriate for them to be secretive, opaque, deliberately deceptive, manipulative, serving not the citizens but, rather, their masters – the corporatists, who assume ownership of the power and control that belongs to the citizens. For our part as citizens, we fail to realise, i.e. *make real,* the fact that we own the government and it is up to each of us to *actively engage* with the day to day affairs of our communities and nation, and *contribute our specific gifts and talents to the common good.*

For those politicians trapped by their corporatist accession, money, material and profit is valued more highly than human life or the integrity of the planet. The problem here is that no *higher value* is generally known, let alone accepted and practised. They and we are conditioned to believe that the values of material acquisition and consumption are the best there are. Until we turn that around, there is a bleak future for the planet and all its inhabitants. Until we are governed by stateswomen and statesmen, life will continue to fragment. Benjamin Disraeli once said that *the world is weary of statesmen whom democracy has degraded into politicians.*

And how did leaders become politicians instead of statesmen and women? Why is material and profit more highly valued than humanity? Because we have allowed – even required – most of our institutions to throw out philosophy and sensible religion, i.e. *re-linked* to the truth about us as we have discussed earlier. In our unconsciousness, we have denied the existence of the spirit – the central essence and executive function of the human being. In doing so, we have thrown out common sense; wisdom! This denial has made way for corporatism to wrest legitimacy from the citizenry, and occupy a position that is unchallenged by both societal leaders – they are more appropriately called followers or managers – and the citizens.

So many wise women and men through the ages have said that money can't be eaten, drunk, breathed, worn, etc. They were the transformed ones; the sophisticated ones - in the true meaning of the word. The corporatists believe they are sophisticated but, in reality, they are unconscious and, thus, well-meaning but ignorant.

Uncommon sense

- Politics created and managed by the unconscious ego will always be dysfunctional and fatally flawed.

- Politics has degenerated into adversarialism, negotiating between interest groups, and the illusion of 'power', rather than it being wise leadership for the common good nationally and internationally.

- Politics, as it is in corporatist societies, is largely irrelevant, impotent and wasteful. It fails miserably to deliver equal quality of life for all, and wise stewardship of the fragile and finite physical environment.

- When anyone speaks against corporatism, they are vilified as 'socialists or communists'. It could be that there is an alternative way that upholds the superior value and integrity of the citizen in *community*. Something called 'communitarianism' – the honouring of all individuals as being of equal worth and ensuring equitable provision for all – is arguably more just and sustainable than any of the common systems.

- Government has degenerated into politics. Whilst government has no control over the financial and, thus, social systems, it is not able to govern.

- Corporatism or democracy? We can't have both, and we have chosen corporatism.

- In a democracy, legitimacy resides with the citizens and not with interest groups of the corporatist paradigm.

Borders and other arbitrary divisions

We hear much emotional, fear-filled talk these days about 'border security' – talk promoted and inflamed by politicians to keep the masses frightened so they will re-elect those whom they are told will keep them safe! And this inhumane, obscene policy and process of so-called border protection has spawned a travesty; a disgraceful, shameful human rights violation. Men, women and children, fleeing for their lives from violence-torn homelands, have been imprisoned by successive corporatist and, thus, undemocratic, Australian governments, without crime, without charge, and without hope of release. Current policies are a national disgrace.

Immigration Ministers and other politicians have continuously mouthed mindless platitudes – lies, actually – about *'saving lives at sea'*. These politicians couldn't care less about the lives of the oppressed, or they would welcome them here and settle them as valued citizens. What politicians care about is to keep their nice, neat portfolios free of unwanted complication, and free from people who are a different colour or creed. These politicians want to maintain the illusion of control in a world that is uncontrollable. These politicians either don't realise, or are avoiding facing the reality, that asylum seekers are their brothers and sisters, equal in worth and every other human measure.

The spin about terrorists coming in by boat has been long since debunked. Somewhere in the region of 97% of all asylum seekers have been confirmed to be genuine refugees.

Yet still we disgracefully imprison them in offshore prisons, and leave them there for years without crime, without charge and without hope. I wonder if that's the way these politicians would like to be treated if the circumstances were reversed. In 2018, the Prime Minister of Australia, on behalf of the Australian people, apologised to the victims of institutional child sexual abuse whilst, at the same time, sanctioning the ongoing abuse of innocent children and adults in offshore detention centres.

In this world we have developed of globalisation, from which the few benefit far more than the many, we are willing to effectively disregard borders for the right to trade and profit, but we are not at all willing to accept the responsibilities that accompany those transactions . We want rights without obligations. We transit arbitrary borders when it suits us, but slam them in place when it does not! Another demonstration of our immaturity as human beings, and our abject failure to realise who we really are and how we really should be behaving.

As discussed earlier, fear drives the actions of the ego – the unconscious, immature human. Throughout history, fear has driven the establishment of arbitrary borders and divisions of all sorts between one people and another. Race, religion, colour, creed, intellect, physical characteristics, difference of any kind produce fear in the ego. The soul feels no such fear because it rightly sees *'the person in front of it as itself, and itself as the person in front of it' (Thich Nhat Hanh)*. For the spirit there are no borders. There is just Oneness.

In this world that we have globalised through technology, trade and mobility, the validity of borders – of nation states, for example – is questionable at least and no longer acceptable at best. Nation states create nationalism – a divisive, often elitist, protectionist milieu. If the world is to remain habitable, if humanity is to survive, the arbitrary divisions of national borders must become a thing of the past. In our daily news bulletins, we hear reports such as *'thirty people died in an horrific bus collision; two of them were Australians'*. Do the 28 non-Australians not matter as much? The tragic reality is that thirty human beings died. Thirty of our brothers and sisters. That is what should matter to us. That is how the spirit experiences such tragedies. Any lesser attitude to the loss is less than fully human, less than appropriately compassionate, less than humble, just and merciful.

So why do we maintain our penchant for arbitrary borders and divisions? I suspect it is again back to the machinations of the proud, frightened, insecure little ego from which most of us operate for most, if not all, of our lives. The ego sees very shallowly. It is only comfortable with circumstances similar to what it sees as its own. Anything different from 'me' is a scary challenge. *Maybe if they are right or OK, I am not'. That is a frightening thought. If their ideas are different from mine, one of us must be* wrong (the ego likes 'black and white, 'right and wrong''). *I can't bear to think it might be 'me', so I'll attack you or your ideas and put them down so that I can again feel in control and right and safe'*.

But, as we've said before, the ego is not who we really are at our true Centre, so it is folly to allow the ego to run the show, and folly not to seek wisdom beyond that shallow little ego. Wisdom that would allow us to see correctly and easily dismantle all borders that currently keep us all in sure 'prisons' of our making. Prisons of suspicion, fear, limitation, sameness, isolation from the fullness of life in all its beauty and variety. Arbitrary borders are human-made – ego made – and have no place in mature humanity. Only by admitting that we don't know what we don't know, and surrendering the illusion of control-by-ego to the true executive – spirit within each of us – will we ever dissolve these life-destroying, arbitrary borders and divisions.

Uncommon sense

- Most borders are arbitrary, artificial, human-created separations of one person or group from another.

- Arbitrary divisions are the creation of the fearful ego/intellect, separating on the basis of race, creed, status, wealth, intellectual ability, physical attractiveness, political stance, social position, etc.

- The human soul in mature humanity recognises no such divisions.

- Borders are created and perpetuated by the powerful minority largely to protect their interests, and what they see as acceptable values.

The trouble with ownership

We human beings like to own stuff. There is something in our nature that drives us to pursue, consume, accumulate and value material things. Although it's normal, and the drive is in each one of us, it is also abnormal in the sense that the drive comes from our lower nature – that persistent ego! More importantly, it is a drive that is destructive of ourselves, each other and this fragile, finite earth. Of course, we return again to the theme of 'who is in control of me; who's calling the shots and directing the intent and effort of my life'? Is it the ego or the spirit? Well, it is probably a combination of the two, but leans too heavily in favour of ego. And that's a disaster. As we mentioned earlier, the ego is that part of us that interacts with the external world for the whole of our lives. And it is essential that it does. And more so early in life. But, for the duration of life – albeit necessarily much-reduced as we mature – the ego must remain intact but in its rightful place as subservient to the direction of the spirit.

It is no mistake that all authentic spiritual paths and sensible religions teach and model non-attachment to the material world – including emotional, spiritual, psychological, physical experiences. Anything and everything can bind us to that which is not helpful to maturing humanity and fullness of life.

The Jesus Christ of history said it like this:

"Do not store up for yourselves treasures on earth where moth and rust destroy, and where thieves break in and steal. But store up for yourself treasure in heaven where moth and rust do not destroy

and thieves do not break in and steal. For where your treasure is, there will your heart be also' (Matthew 6:19-21). He also said, *'Love the Lord your God with all your heart, with all your soul, with all your mind and with all your strength, and love your neighbour as yourself'* (Mark 12:30-31). Notice he said 'love', an outward giving, not 'gather to yourself'. Notice also he focused on God first, neighbour and self next – not me first, middle and last. Notice also he sequenced *'heart, soul'* before *'mind and strength'*. We could assume there's a few clues here. First, our heart and life energy needs to be spent on what is worthy in life. That means first we must *love* – God, others, self, the earth.

Secondly, we need to be careful to engage with our heart and soul before our mind and strength. To fail to focus on God first – and with heart and soul first – is to risk spending our life energy on matters of the mind and body. And that usually means focusing predominantly on the material aspects of life. That includes information and knowledge which is not necessarily wisdom. And it generally means production, consumption, accumulation, self-gratification and neglect of all else. We only have to look around at the world we have created to see the destructiveness and meaninglessness of much of our current focus and values.

Buddhism teaches that it is best to have few possessions and to use those for the betterment of others. Within Hinduism, wealth is regarded as positive if pursued within limits, if it provides charity for those in need, and the holder of the wealth is not attached to it; i.e. they could take it or leave it with equanimity.

Now, there is nothing wrong with capital, material goods, personal creativity, development of personal gifts and talents, scientific discoveries, technological advancement, careful use of the earth's resources, deep and intimate relationships, etc., unless we become attached to them. Unless they become all consuming. Unless they cause us to *take from*, rather than *give to*, life. Unless they become a higher priority in our lives than *love* in all that that means. And we're not talking Hollywood here. We're not talking sensual and sexual desire and gratification. We're talking concern for others and the earth. We're talking moderate use and conservation of resources. We're talking giving *of* self before giving *to* self. We're talking living in the knowledge that my life doesn't belong to me, it belongs to life! I have been given gifts in order to express them fully and give them back to the world that needs every gift of every person and creature. It is *good for me* to give of myself! When I am giving of my *gifts*, not only am I my best self, I am my most personally-enjoyed self!

The other salutary thing about possessions is that we can't actually possess anything. The material world remains long after we have departed! But we can be possessed by things. That is our real danger. That is destroying the world. We are fighting wars about it. We are denying billions of our brothers and sisters access to the basic requirements for a life of dignity. Families are tearing each other apart in their fight over deceased estates. The earth is being torn apart in our insatiable desire for personal pleasure.

Why is this love we're talking about to be our first, greatest and enduring consideration? It's simple. Loving is good for ME! For us! Loving fulfils! Loving is good for the earth and all its inhabitants. In loving, we experience receiving far more than we give. Loving makes life work.

Of course, we don't love because we realise it's good for us. We love because it is the right and best way to be in life. The bonus is that it is also good for ME! Nothing to lose, everything to gain, and for everyone. Love sees you as myself and myself as you. Love is unable to withhold what it has to give. Love gives recklessly and never runs out!

Humanity desperately needs to be realigned to this love of God, other, self and the earth with heart, soul, mind and strength. Nothing else will allow a future worth living.

Secondly, ownership is an illusion. Because we are finite, we can't hold any 'thing' indefinitely. We can't properly 'own' anything. All we can do is use things for a time, and then let go of them. And let go of everything we must. If we don't – if we attach to anything of this world – we will live shallow lives characterised by fear. There may be the appearance that all is well but, not far beneath the surface, the reality is less than ideal.

Uncommon sense

- The human drive to pursue, consume, accumulate and value material things comes from our lower nature – ego.

- This human drive is destructive of ourselves, each other and the earth, as we attach to things rather than to life

- All authentic spiritual paths and sensible religions teach and model non-attachment to anything and everything.

- Life works best when we pursue that which is incorruptible and eternal. Store our treasure in 'heaven', that mysterious and greatest reality permeating and energising the entire universe including ourselves; that reality *within* ourselves!

- We are to treasure love above all else, and with the heart and soul before, but including, the mind and strength.

- There is nothing wrong with material goods necessary to sustain life. What makes material goods wrong is our attachment to them.

- Our drive to 'own' is tearing apart ourselves, families, communities, eco-systems. We fight wars over the illusion of ownership.

Wealth and Greed

Following our brief discussion of ownership is the distortion – the perversion – of our interaction with material goods: wealth and its associated evil, greed.

It has been said (2 Corinthians 8:15) that if we live correctly, *'those who have much will have no excess, and those who have little will have no lack'*! In our wealthy western nations, that statement is thought treasonous by many. They will protest 'we are a democracy... we have a right to the benefits of free enterprise and making personal profit... what's wrong with working hard and getting ahead?' 'Ahead of whom?', we might ask. And the inconvenient truth – the unpleasant answer – is 'ahead of the vast majority of humanity'. They are our brothers and sisters in our own communities and around the world for whom the daily struggle is for the basics of survival. And that's mere survival without human dignity!

'What's wrong with personal wealth?', we may ask. What's wrong is that wealth provides physical comfort. It makes my life sensually more pleasant. I like that! I like it so much I don't want to lose it. I get to depend on it. I attach great importance to it. I remember what it was like without it and want to make sure I always have plenty. So I stack it up, protect it, insure it, guard it in every way possible. I am very reluctant to share any of it with anyone. If I can acquire it, so can everyone else!

Oh, really?

I have become greedy!

That's what's wrong with wealth. It seduces me, perverts me, makes you and me adversaries. It silences the inner voice of my spirit. It possesses me. And I am lost!

A bit dramatic, perhaps? Not in the slightest! Wealth is pernicious, becomes malignant and, if untreated, terminal! Not only of the wealthy, but of the earth which is home to all creatures and, more tragically, to the human spirit separated from its source and origin in the eternal spirit mystery we may call God. In and of itself, however, personal wealth is *benign* and, if employed in the service of humankind, becomes good. As the wealth pours in to the one, it is poured out to the many.

Of course, the corporatists argue that wealth creation is good for the economy. That's a convenient lie that has been so diligently propagated that it is widely believed even by those it's destroying; the citizens of the world. The wealthy *think* it's good for them, but it's not. It may make them physically and psychologically comfortable, but it actually destroys them by separating them from their true Selves – their spirits – and from their many brothers and sisters who are denied access to the same circumstances.

Wealth never trickles down. It surges up – for the few!

And those few are the ones who own and control the financial and, thus, social circumstances of the citizenry. You and me. And the governments who accept the lie that private ownership of financial services and systems is the only way it can be – are complicit in the lie. Governments who exclude themselves from the making and changing of monetary policy, are not governing; they are 'politicking'! They are colluding with the corporatist destroyers of nations, and fooling themselves that they are actually governing.

We are encouraged by Wisdom to *'seek first the kingdom of God and righteousness, and all other things will be added to you'* (Matthew 6:33). The wisest women and men of all history and all authentic, sensible religion and spirituality affirm that truth. The kingdom that is not of this world is the source and destiny of life in all its fullness. And that kingdom is *within* each of us if only we will open ourselves to seek it, immerse ourselves in it and, in so doing, begin to function as conscious, mature, loving human beings.

Uncommon sense

- Wealth produces physical comfort. It starts out pleasant, become desirable, then necessary, essential, and I am 'hooked'. My life is now controlled by my senses rather than my wisdom.
- Wealth perverts my deepest humanity, makes adversaries of women and men, silences the inner voice of my spirit.
- Wealth, untempered by wisdom, produces greed.
- Wealth is pernicious, malignant and, if untreated, terminal not only of the wealthy, but of the earth which is home to all creatures, and to the spirit of humankind – the central and indispensable human characteristic.
- We have accepted the lie that wealth creation is good for the nation. It is not even good for the wealthy.
- We are exhorted by Jesus and others voices of wisdom throughout history to *'seek first the kingdom of God and righteousness, and all other things will be added to you'*. (Matthew 6:33). That is, we'll be truly wealthy!

Conclusion

It seems there are two types of *sense*.

One is accepted by many of us generally as 'normal' and the only one there is. That *sense*, if analysed a little, often proves to be *senseless*. It largely focuses on the self, is blind, consumes, wastes, pollutes, hoards, divides, alienates, differentiates, judges, condemns, attacks, destroys, avoids, complicates, controls and is trapped. That 'sense' is the sense of human unconsciousness. The inflated, unbridled ego. Our essential but inferior capacity.

The second type of sense is the sense that is no longer commonly known, accepted and practised. This sense comes from the Centre or spirit of the human person, and renews the mind. This sense – tragically uncommon as it is – is true sense. Wisdom. It sees correctly. It is other-focused, conserves, protects, purifies, shares, unites, includes, embraces, is simple, careful, compassionate, surrendered and free. It arises from the inner fount of Love – our Centre, spirit, the truth about us – that which a Christian might call 'the Spirit of God' or the 'kingdom of God within'. A person of Hindu faith might call that part 'Atman', a Buddhist may use the term 'Buddha nature'. Every sensible religion has a way of acknowledging, speaking about and engaging with that inner and universal mystery reality. Where there is Love, there is God, truth, life.

The situation of this world really is serious. Life as we know it – not just for humanity but for all life forms on earth – is in serious jeopardy.

And our situation is also really hopeful. For life on earth to survive – for there to be a future anything like life as we know it – uncommon sense has to be made common again. Uncommon sense is to *return* to the rejected truth of our divine humanity; our spiritual inner essence. That mysterious, indescribable Spirit of Divine Love, by and through and in which all things are mysteriously formed and hold together. To *return* is to regain life the way it was intended. The only way real life – abundant and delightful life for all – is possible. It is the way of the *empowering personal and corporate surrender* and, paradoxically, true freedom, versus the way of disabling control and personal and corporate entrapment and destruction. It is the way of leadership; the way of governance. It is the way of recognising, developing, and overseeing monetary and social policy that is actually for the common good. It is the way of becoming democratic. It is common sense!

We can – we *must* – choose and work to make uncommon sense common again.

About the author

John White was raised in Mount Barker, Western Australia, in a hard-working family, and attended the local state school. Although he achieved tolerably well, his interest was more in 'doing' than in academic pursuits. He excelled at athletics, music and practical arts, and left school at age 16 to work on the small family farm for several years.

A downturn in the wool industry forced him to seek other employment and he found work in the local radio station, 6VA Albany, becoming the breakfast announcer within a few months. During that time he also began singing as a guest artist in pubs and night clubs, and attained Private Pilot License for fixed- wing aircraft. Wanting to bring the radio station into the twentieth century, after about a year he introduced some 'personality' into his show. As management hadn't authorised the changes, he was summarily dismissed!

Returning to tertiary studies he trained at what is now Edith Cowan University, became a secondary teacher, and taught for 12 years. Coming into contact with troubled youngsters led John to study psychotherapy, counselling, and clinical supervision, and he worked in that field for more than thirty years.

John is married to Jennifer, his first and only wife, and they have two adult children – Emma and Benjamin. Emma and her husband Alan have three sons, Hamish, Nathan and Ian.

John and Jennifer live in the small country town of Toodyay, about an hour east of Perth, Western Australia.

John is active in promoting justice socially, environmentally and politically.

www.ingramcontent.com/pod-product-compliance
Lightning Source LLC
Chambersburg PA
CBHW052017290426
44112CB00014B/2272